KitchenAid®
STAND MIXER
COOKBOOK

Publications International, Ltd.

Contents

Getting the Most from Your KitchenAid® Stand Mixer

You count on your KitchenAid stand mixer to mix cookies, whip egg whites and knead bread dough, but there are countless other ways it can make cooking and baking easier, better and more enjoyable. Every stand mixer comes with three basic attachments: the flat beater, wire whip and dough hook. Here are some tips on making the best use of all three.

 Flat Beater

The flat beater is probably the attachment you use most. It's perfect for creaming butter and sugar, combining ingredients, beating cake batters and many other basic tasks. Use it for: cakes, creamed frostings, candies, cookies, pie pastry, biscuits, quick breads, meat loaf and mashed potatoes.

ATTACHMENT HUB

Turn your stand mixer into a culinary center. The hub powers over 12 optional accessories, such as a food grinder, spiralizer, pasta maker set and more. Simply remove the multipurpose attachment hub to allow for easy installation of optional attachments.

Cutting Butter or Shortening into Flour

Your KitchenAid stand mixer makes short work of short doughs, including biscuits, pie pastry and scones without overworking the dough. Cut chilled butter or shortening into pieces and add it to the flour in the mixer bowl. Turn the flat beater to low and mix until the mixture resembles coarse crumbs (or the texture specified for a particular recipe). You'll keep your hands clean and the butter cold, which makes for a lighter and flakier result.

Wire Whip

The wire whip is the attachment to reach for when air needs to be incorporated into a mixture. This includes recipes that call for beaten egg whites, like soufflés, angel food cakes, sponge cakes and French macarons. The whip is also perfect for making mayonnaise or boiled frostings and, of course, for whipping cream.

How to Whip Egg Whites

It's easiest to separate egg yolks from whites when the eggs are cold, however, room temperature whites achieve greater volume. Be careful to keep all of the yolk, or any other fat, out of the egg whites. A drop or two of yolk is enough to prevent proper whipping.

Place the room temperature whites in a clean, dry mixer bowl. (Even a tiny bit of leftover grease in the bowl could prevent the whites from achieving volume.) Attach the wire whip. Whip, gradually increasing the speed to high. Beat until the egg whites reach the desired stage.

Foamy or Frothy: Large uneven air bubbles form.

Soft Peaks: Whites form a peak when lifted, but tips fall over when the whip is removed.

Stiff, Shiny Peaks: Sharp stiff peaks remain even when the whip is removed. Egg whites are glossy.

Sweetened Whipped Cream

- 1½ **cups heavy whipping cream**
- ¼ **cup powdered sugar**
- ½ **teaspoon vanilla**

Pour cream into bowl of KitchenAid stand mixer. Attach bowl and wire whip to mixer. To avoid splashing, begin whipping on Stir speed and gradually increase to speed 8. When cream forms soft peaks, add powdered sugar and vanilla. Continue whipping to desired consistency. (Do not overbeat or cream will become grainy.)

Tip: For best results, freeze the mixer bowl and wire whip 15 minutes before whipping the cream.

MAKES ABOUT 3 CUPS. MAY BE DOUBLED.

Types of Cream

Labels on containers of cream can be mystifying. Here are some definitions.

Light Cream (18 to 30% butterfat): Generally the same as half-and-half. Will only whip if it contains 30% butterfat.

Whipping Cream (30% butterfat): Will whip and thicken, but not as well as heavy whipping cream.

Heavy Whipping Cream (36 to 38% butterfat): Whips up well and holds its shape. Doubles in volume when whipped.

Pasteurized vs. Ultra-Pasteurized: Ultra-pasteurized whipping cream has been heated to a higher temperature than regular pasteurized cream in order to extend its shelf life. Ultra-pasteurized cream takes longer to whip and will not retain peaks like pasteurized cream.

Dough Hook

The dough hook is a breadmaker's best friend. Use it for mixing and kneading yeast doughs including breads, rolls, coffee cakes and buns.

Bread Basics

Yeast is alive. Use a kitchen thermometer to check liquids. Temperatures that are too high can kill the yeast and low temperatures will slow yeast growth and the time required for bread to rise.

Most bread recipes call for a range in the amount of flour. You'll know you've added enough when dough clings to the hook and cleans the side of the bowl. Some dough, especially when made with whole grains, may not form a ball on the hook. As long as the hook is making contact with the dough, it is being kneaded. Always keep the speed low while using the dough hook. Refer to the stand mixer instruction book for details.

Rising times vary due to any number of factors, including the temperature and humidity level in your kitchen. To judge whether dough has doubled, press into it lightly with your fingers. If the indentations remain, the dough has risen enough.

A GUIDE TO MIXER SPEEDS	
1	Stir
2–3	Low
4–5	Medium-low
6–7	Medium
8–9	Medium-high
10	High

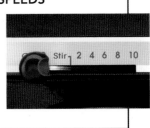

Cookies

Madeleines

MAKES ABOUT 44 CAKES

2½ **cups cake flour**

 2 **teaspoons baking powder**

 ¾ **cup sugar**

 2 **vanilla pods, seeds scraped *or* 2 teaspoons vanilla extract**

 Pinch of salt

 6 **eggs**

 2 **teaspoons grated lime peel**

 3 **tablespoons fresh lime juice**

1⅓ **cups (2 sticks plus 5 tablespoons) unsalted butter, melted**

 ¼ **cup honey**

1 Sift flour and baking powder into small bowl. Combine sugar, vanilla seeds and pinch of salt in bowl of KitchenAid stand mixer. Attach bowl and wire whip to mixer. Turn mixer to speed 4; add eggs, one at a time, mixing 1 minute after each addition. Increase to speed 6; whip 1 minute or until light and frothy. Scrap bottom and side of bowl.

2 Turn mixer to Stir speed. Gradually add flour mixture; mix 30 seconds or just until combined. Scrape bowl. Add lime peel and juice; mix on Stir speed just until combined. With mixer running, add melted butter and honey; mix 20 seconds or until soft dough forms.

3 Transfer dough to large pastry bag or resealable food storage bag with corner cut off. Seal and let dough rest in refrigerator 30 minutes. Meanwhile, preheat oven to 400°F. Grease and flour madeleine pans.

4 Pipe about 1½ tablespoons chilled batter into prepared pans. Bake 8 to 10 minutes. Cool in pan 1 minute. Remove to wire rack; cool completely.

Chocolate Variation: Omit lime peel and juice. Reduce cake flour by ¼ cup and add ¼ cup unsweetened cocoa powder.

Chocolate Raspberry Thumbprints

MAKES ABOUT 4½ DOZEN COOKIES

1½ **cups (3 sticks) unsalted butter, softened**

1 **cup granulated sugar**

1 **egg**

1 **teaspoon vanilla**

3 **cups all-purpose flour**

¼ **cup unsweetened cocoa powder**

½ **teaspoon salt**

1 **cup mini semisweet chocolate chips (optional)**

Powdered sugar (optional)

⅔ **cup raspberry preserves**

1 Preheat oven to 350°F. Grease cookie sheets or line with parchment paper.

2 Combine butter and granulated sugar in bowl of KitchenAid stand mixer. Attach bowl and flat beater to mixer. Turn mixer to speed 6; beat 3 minutes until very smooth. Add egg and vanilla; beat until light and fluffy. Scrape bottom and side of bowl. With mixer running on Stir speed, gradually add flour, cocoa and salt until well blended. Stir in mini chocolate chips, if desired.

3 Shape level tablespoonfuls of dough into balls. Place 2 inches apart on prepared cookie sheets. Make deep indentation in center of each ball with thumb.

4 Bake 10 to 12 minutes or just until set. Cool on cookie sheets 2 minutes. Remove to wire racks; cool completely.

5 Sprinkle cookies with powdered sugar, if desired. Fill centers with raspberry preserves. Store between layers of waxed paper in airtight containers.

Giant Chocolate Chip Walnut Cookies

MAKES 1 DOZEN LARGE COOKIES

1¾ cups all-purpose flour

1 cup cake flour

1 teaspoon baking powder

¾ teaspoon baking soda

¾ teaspoon salt

1 cup (2 sticks) cold unsalted butter, cut into cubes

¾ cup packed brown sugar

½ cup granulated sugar

2 eggs

1 teaspoon vanilla

2 cups coarsely chopped walnuts

2 cups semisweet chocolate chips

1 Preheat oven to 400°F. Line two cookie sheets with parchment paper. Position oven rack in center of oven.

2 Whisk all-purpose flour, cake flour, baking powder, baking soda and salt in medium bowl. Combine butter, brown sugar and granulated sugar in bowl of KitchenAid stand mixer. Attach bowl and flat beater to mixer. Turn mixer to speed 6; beat 1 to 2 minutes or until smooth and creamy. Add eggs one at time, beating well after each addition. Beat in vanilla. Scrape bottom and side of bowl. With mixer running on Stir speed, gradually add flour mixture just until blended. Stir in walnuts and chocolate chips until blended.

3 Shape dough into 12 mounds slightly smaller than a tennis ball (about 4 ounces each); arrange 2 inches apart on prepared cookie sheets (six cookies per sheet).

4 Bake one sheet at a time about 12 minutes or until tops are light golden brown. (Cover loosely with foil if cookies are browning too quickly.) Remove cookie sheet to wire rack; cool cookies on cookie sheet 15 minutes. (Cookies will continue to bake while standing.) Serve warm.

Gingerbread Whoopie Pies

MAKES 12 SERVINGS

COOKIES

- **3 cups all-purpose flour**
- **2 teaspoons ground cinnamon**
- **2 teaspoons ground ginger**
- **1 teaspoon salt**
- **1 teaspoon ground allspice**
- **¾ teaspoon baking soda**
- **½ teaspoon baking powder**
- **¾ cup (1½ sticks) unsalted butter, softened**
- **½ cup packed dark brown sugar**
- **½ cup molasses**
- **2 eggs**
- **2 teaspoons vanilla**
- **½ cup buttermilk**

MARSHMALLOW FILLING

- **2 teaspoons unflavored gelatin**
- **½ cup cold water, divided**
- **¾ cup granulated sugar**
- **½ cup light corn syrup**
- **¼ teaspoon salt**

1 Whisk flour, cinnamon, ginger, 1 teaspoon salt, allspice, baking soda and baking powder in medium bowl. Combine butter, brown sugar and molasses in bowl of KitchenAid stand mixer. Attach bowl and flat beater to mixer. Turn to speed 4; mix 2 minutes or until well blended. Add eggs and vanilla; mix until well blended. Scrape bottom and side of bowl.

2 Turn mixer to Stir speed; add flour mixture alternately with buttermilk, beginning and ending with flour mixture. Mix just until combined. Transfer to medium bowl. Cover and refrigerate 2 hours.

3 For filling, combine gelatin and ¼ cup cold water in clean mixer bowl. Attach bowl and wire whip to mixer. Let stand while preparing syrup.

4 Combine remaining ¼ cup cold water, granulated sugar, corn syrup and ¼ teaspoon salt in small heavy saucepan. Clip candy thermometer to side of pan. Cook without stirring over medium-high heat to 240°F.

5 Preheat oven to 350°F. Turn mixer to Speed 8. Slowly pour hot syrup into mixer bowl toward side of bowl. Whip about 10 minutes or until mixture is white and fluffy.

6 Line cookie sheets with parchment paper. Using 1½ ounce scoop, portion 24 cookies 2 inches apart onto prepared cookie sheets.

7 Bake 10 to 12 minutes or until lightly browned and edges are crisp. Remove to wire rack; cool completely. Spread filling over flat side of half of cookies. Top with remaining cookies.

Chocolate Coconut Toffee Cookies

MAKES 1 DOZEN LARGE COOKIES

½ cup all-purpose flour

¼ teaspoon baking powder

¼ teaspoon salt

1 package (12 ounces) semisweet chocolate chips, divided

¼ cup (½ stick) unsalted butter, cut into small pieces

¾ cup packed brown sugar

2 eggs

1 teaspoon vanilla

1½ cups flaked coconut

1 cup toffee baking bits

½ cup bittersweet chocolate chips

1 Preheat oven to 350°F. Line cookie sheets with parchment paper. Whisk flour, baking powder and salt in small bowl.

2 Combine 1 cup semisweet chocolate chips and butter in medium microwavable bowl. Microwave on HIGH 1 minute; stir. Microwave at additional 30-second intervals until mixture is melted and smooth, stirring after each interval. Or melt in medium heavy saucepan over very low heat until melted and smooth.

3 Combine brown sugar, eggs and vanilla in bowl of KitchenAid stand mixer. Attach bowl and flat beater to mixer. Turn to speed 6; beat 2 minutes or until creamy. Beat in chocolate mixture until well blended. Scrape bottom and side of bowl. With mixer running on Stir speed, gradually add flour mixture just until blended. Stir in coconut, toffee bits and remaining 1 cup semisweet chocolate chips. Drop dough by heaping ⅓ cupfuls 3 inches apart onto prepared cookie sheets. Flatten with spatula into 3½-inch circles.

4 Bake 15 to 17 minutes or until edges are firm to the touch. Cool on cookie sheets 2 minutes. Slide parchment paper and cookies onto wire racks; cool completely.

5 Place bittersweet chocolate chips in small microwavable bowl. Microwave on HIGH 30 seconds; stir. Microwave at additional 30-second intervals until melted and smooth, stirring after each interval. Drizzle over cookies with fork. Let stand until set.

Sea Salt Chocolate Chunk Cookies

MAKES ABOUT 20 COOKIES

1½ **cups all-purpose flour**

¾ **teaspoon baking soda**

¾ **teaspoon smoked or regular sea salt**

½ **cup (1 stick) unsalted butter, at room temperature**

¼ **cup packed dark brown sugar**

¼ **cup granulated sugar**

1 **egg**

1 **teaspoon vanilla**

8 **ounces semisweet chocolate, chopped**

1 Whisk flour, baking soda and salt in medium bowl. Combine butter and sugars in bowl of KitchenAid stand mixer. Attach bowl and flat beater to mixer. Turn to speed 6; beat 3 minutes or until pale and fluffy. Add egg and vanilla; mix until well blended. Scrape bottom and side of bowl.

2 Turn mixer to Stir speed. Gradually add flour mixture; mix 30 seconds or just until combined. Add chocolate; stir 10 seconds or until just combined. Transfer dough to medium bowl; cover and refrigerate at least 2 hours or overnight.

3 Preheat oven to 350°F. Line cookie sheets with parchment paper. Use 1½-tablespoon cookie scoop to portion cookie dough 2 inches apart onto prepared cookie sheets.

4 Bake 9 to 10 minutes or until edges are golden brown. Remove to wire racks; cool completely.

Mexican Hot Chocolate Cookies

MAKES ABOUT 3½ DOZEN COOKIES

COOKIES

2½ cups all-purpose flour

½ cup Dutch process cocoa powder

2 teaspoons cream of tartar

1 teaspoon baking soda

1 teaspoon salt

½ teaspoon baking powder

½ teaspoon ground nutmeg

¼ teaspoon ground red pepper

¼ teaspoon black pepper

1 cup (2 sticks) unsalted butter, softened

½ cup granulated sugar

⅓ cup packed dark brown sugar

2 eggs

1 teaspoon vanilla

1 cup milk chocolate chips or chunks

1 ounce bittersweet chocolate, grated

TOPPING

½ cup granulated sugar

2 teaspoons ground cinnamon

1 Preheat oven to 375°F. Line cookie sheets with parchment paper. Whisk flour, cocoa, cream of tartar, baking soda, salt, baking powder, nutmeg, ground red pepper and black pepper in medium bowl.

2 Place butter, ½ cup granulated sugar and brown sugar in bowl of KitchenAid stand mixer. Attach bowl and flat beater to mixer. Turn mixer to speed 2; mix 20 seconds. Increase to speed 6; beat 3 to 4 minutes or until light and fluffy. With mixer running on Stir speed, add eggs one at a time, beating 1 minute after each addition. Beat in vanilla. Scrape bottom and side of bowl.

3 With mixer running on Stir speed, add flour mixture in three additions. Stir in milk chocolate chips and grated chocolate with spatula until well blended.

4 Combine ½ cup granulated sugar and cinnamon in medium bowl. Shape dough by tablespoonfuls into balls. Roll in cinnamon-sugar mixture; place 2 inches apart on prepared cookie sheets.

5 Bake 8 to 10 minutes or until edges are set and tops are puffed and cracked, rotating baking sheets halfway through baking. Cool on cookie sheets 5 minutes. Remove to wire racks; cool completely.

Black and White Cookies

MAKES 1½ DOZEN COOKIES

COOKIES

- 2 **cups all-purpose flour**
- 1 **tablespoon cornstarch**
- ¾ **teaspoon baking soda**
- ½ **teaspoon salt**
- ¾ **cup (1½ sticks) unsalted butter, softened**
- 1 **cup granulated sugar**
- 2 **eggs**
- 1 **teaspoon vanilla**
- ½ **teaspoon grated lemon peel**
- ⅔ **cup buttermilk**

ICINGS

- 3½ **cups powdered sugar, divided**
- 3 **tablespoons plus 3 teaspoons boiling water, divided**
- 1 **tablespoon fresh lemon juice**
- 2 **teaspoons corn syrup, divided**
- ½ **teaspoon vanilla**
- 3 **ounces unsweetened chocolate, melted**

1 Preheat oven to 350°F. Line cookie sheets with parchment paper. Whisk flour, cornstarch, baking soda and salt in small bowl.

2 Combine butter and granulated sugar in bowl of KitchenAid stand mixer. Attach bowl and flat beater to mixer. Turn mixer to speed 8; beat 5 minutes or until light and fluffy. Beat in eggs, one at a time; beat in 1 teaspoon vanilla and lemon peel. Scrape bottom and side of bowl. Turn mixer to Stir speed; add flour mixture alternately with buttermilk, beating until blended after each addition. Scrape bowl with spatula and stir several times to bring dough together. Using dampened hands, shape 3 tablespoons of dough into a ball for each cookie. Place on prepared cookie sheets 3 inches apart.

3 Bake 13 to 15 minutes or until tops are puffed and edges are lightly browned. Cool on cookie sheets 1 minute. Remove to wire racks; trim any crispy browned edges, if desired. Cool completely.

4 Place 2 cups powdered sugar in small bowl; whisk in 1 tablespoon boiling water, lemon juice and 1 teaspoon corn syrup until smooth and well blended. If necessary, add additional 1 teaspoon water to make smooth, thick and spreadable glaze. Spread icing over half of each cookie; place on wire rack or waxed paper to set.

5 Place remaining 1½ cups powdered sugar in another small bowl; whisk in 2 tablespoons boiling water, remaining 1 teaspoon corn syrup and ¼ teaspoon vanilla. Whisk in chocolate until smooth and well blended. If necessary, add additional 1 to 2 teaspoons water to make smooth, thick and spreadable glaze. Spread icing on other side of each cookie. Place on wire rack; let stand until set. Cookies are best the day they're made.

Super Chocolate Cookies

MAKES ABOUT 20 COOKIES

2 cups all-purpose flour

⅓ cup unsweetened cocoa powder

1 teaspoon baking soda

½ teaspoon salt

1⅓ cups packed brown sugar

1 cup (2 sticks) unsalted butter, softened

2 eggs

2 teaspoons vanilla

1 cup candy-coated chocolate pieces

1 cup dried cranberries, dried cherries and/or raisins

¾ cup salted peanuts

1 Preheat oven to 350°F. Whisk flour, cocoa, baking soda and salt in medium bowl.

2 Place brown sugar and butter in bowl of KitchenAid stand mixer. Attach bowl and flat beater to mixer. Turn mixer to speed 6; beat 5 minutes or until light and fluffy. Add eggs one at a time, beating well after each addition. Beat in vanilla. Scrape bottom and side of bowl. With mixer running on Stir speed, gradually add flour mixture just until blended. Stir in chocolate pieces, cranberries and peanuts.

3 Drop dough by ¼ cupfuls 3 inches apart onto ungreased cookie sheets. Flatten slightly with fingertips. Bake 10 minutes or until almost set. Cool on cookie sheets 2 minutes. Remove to wire racks; cool completely.

Dark Chocolate Dreams

MAKES 14 COOKIES

½ cup all-purpose flour

¾ teaspoon espresso powder or ½ teaspoon ground cinnamon

½ teaspoon baking powder

½ teaspoon salt

16 ounces bittersweet chocolate, coarsely chopped

¼ cup (½ stick) unsalted butter

1½ cups sugar

3 eggs

1 teaspoon vanilla

1 package (12 ounces) white chocolate chips

1 cup dark chocolate chips or chopped toasted pecans

1 Preheat oven to 350°F. Grease cookie sheets or line with parchment paper. Whisk flour, espresso powder, baking powder and salt in small bowl.

2 Combine chocolate and butter in large heavy saucepan. Heat over very low heat until melted and smooth, stirring frequently. Or combine in large microwavable bowl; microwave on HIGH 2 minutes. Stir and microwave 1 to 2 minutes, stirring after 1 minute, or until chocolate is melted. Cool slightly.

3 Place sugar, eggs and vanilla in bowl of KitchenAid stand mixer. Attach bowl and flat beater to mixer. Turn to speed 8; beat 6 minutes until very thick and mixture turns pale color. Reduce to Stir speed; gradually beat in chocolate mixture until well blended. Gradually beat in flour mixture until blended. Scrape bottom and side of bowl. Fold in white chocolate chips and dark chocolate chips with spatula.

4 Drop dough by level ⅓ cupfuls 3 inches apart onto prepared cookie sheets. Flatten into 4-inch circles with moistened fingers.

5 Bake 12 minutes or just until firm and surface begins to crack. *Do not overbake.* Cool on cookie sheets 5 minutes. Remove to wire racks; cool completely.

Bar Cookies

Double Chocolate Dream Bars

MAKES 2 TO 3 DOZEN BARS

2¼ **cups all-purpose flour, divided**

1 **cup (2 sticks) unsalted butter, softened**

¾ **cup powdered sugar, plus additional for garnish**

⅓ **cup unsweetened cocoa powder**

½ **teaspoon salt**

2 **cups granulated sugar**

4 **eggs**

4 **ounces unsweetened chocolate, melted**

1 Preheat oven to 350°F. Line 13×9-inch baking pan with parchment paper.

2 Combine 2 cups flour, butter, ¾ cup powdered sugar, cocoa and salt in bowl of KitchenAid stand mixer. Attach bowl and flat beater to mixer. Turn to Stir speed; mix until blended. Increase to speed 4; beat until well blended and stiff dough forms. Press firmly into prepared pan. Bake 15 to 20 minutes or just until set. *Do not overbake.*

3 Meanwhile, combine remaining ¼ cup flour and granulated sugar in clean mixer bowl. Add eggs and melted chocolate; beat on speed 8 until well blended. Pour over crust.

4 Bake 25 minutes or until center is firm to the touch. Cool completely in pan on wire rack. Sprinkle with additional powdered sugar, if desired. Remove from pan using parchment; cut into bars.

Pumpkin Cheesecake Bars

MAKES ABOUT 2 DOZEN BARS

1½ **cups gingersnap crumbs, plus additional for garnish**

6 **tablespoons (¾ stick) unsalted butter, melted**

12 **ounces cream cheese, softened**

¼ **cup plus 2 tablespoons sugar, divided**

2½ **teaspoons vanilla, divided**

2 **eggs**

1¼ **cups canned pumpkin**

1 **teaspoon ground cinnamon**

¼ **teaspoon ground ginger**

¼ **teaspoon ground nutmeg**

¼ **teaspoon ground cloves**

1 **cup sour cream**

1 Preheat oven to 325°F. Spray 13×9-inch baking pan with nonstick cooking spray.

2 Combine 1½ cups gingersnap crumbs and butter in small bowl; mix well. Press into prepared pan. Bake 10 minutes.

3 Meanwhile, place cream cheese, ¼ cup sugar and 1½ teaspoons vanilla in bowl of KitchenAid stand mixer. Attach bowl and flat beater to mixer. Turn to speed 4; mix 1 minute or until smooth. Beat in eggs one at a time. Scrape bottom and side of bowl. Add pumpkin, cinnamon, ginger, nutmeg and cloves; mix on speed 2 until well blended. Pour evenly over hot crust.

4 Bake 40 minutes. Whisk sour cream, remaining 2 tablespoons sugar and 1 teaspoon vanilla in small bowl until blended. Remove cheesecake from oven; spread sour cream mixture evenly over top. Bake 5 minutes. Turn off oven; open door halfway and let cheesecake cool completely in oven. Refrigerate at least 2 hours. Cut into bars; garnish with additional gingersnap crumbs.

Lemon Squares

MAKES 2 TO 3 DOZEN SQUARES

CRUST

- **1 cup (2 sticks) unsalted butter, softened**
- **½ cup granulated sugar**
- **½ teaspoon salt**
- **2 cups all-purpose flour**

FILLING

- **3 cups granulated sugar**
- **1 cup all-purpose flour**
- **4 eggs plus 2 egg yolks, at room temperature**
- **⅔ cup fresh lemon juice**
- **2 tablespoons grated lemon peel**
- **½ teaspoon baking powder**
- **Powdered sugar**

1 Combine butter, ½ cup granulated sugar and salt in bowl of KitchenAid stand mixer. Attach bowl and flat beater to mixer. Turn to speed 6; beat 3 minutes or until light and fluffy. Scrape bottom and side of bowl. With mixer running on Stir speed, gradually add 2 cups flour just until blended.

2 Grease 13×9-inch baking pan. Press dough into prepared pan, building edges up ½ inch on all sides. Refrigerate 20 minutes.

3 Preheat oven to 350°F. Bake crust 15 to 20 minutes or until very lightly browned. Cool on wire rack.

4 Combine 3 cups granulated sugar, 1 cup flour, eggs and egg yolks, lemon juice, lemon peel and baking powder in clean mixer bowl. Attach bowl and wire whip to stand mixer. Turn to speed 4 and mix until well blended. Pour over crust.

5 Bake 30 to 35 minutes until filling is set. Cool completely in pan on wire rack. Cut into squares; sprinkle with powdered sugar.

Shortbread Turtle Cookie Bars

MAKES ABOUT 4½ DOZEN BARS

1¼ cups (2½ sticks) unsalted butter, softened, divided

1 cup all-purpose flour

1 cup old-fashioned oats

1¼ cups packed brown sugar, divided

1 teaspoon ground cinnamon

½ teaspoon salt

1½ cups chopped pecans

6 ounces bittersweet or semisweet chocolate, finely chopped

4 ounces white chocolate, finely chopped

1 Preheat oven to 350°F.

2 Place ½ cup butter in bowl of KitchenAid stand mixer. Attach bowl and flat beater to mixer. Turn mixer to speed 6; beat 2 minutes or until very smooth. Add flour, oats, ¾ cup brown sugar, cinnamon and salt; mix on Stir speed until coarse crumbs form. Press firmly into ungreased 13×9-inch baking pan.

3 Combine remaining ¾ cup butter and ¾ cup brown sugar in medium saucepan. Cook over medium heat, stirring constantly until mixture comes to a boil. Boil 1 minute without stirring. Remove from heat; stir in pecans. Pour evenly over crust.

4 Bake 18 to 22 minutes or until caramel begins to bubble. Immediately sprinkle with bittersweet and white chocolate; swirl (do not spread) with knife after 45 seconds to 1 minute or when slightly softened. Cool completely in pan on wire rack. Cut into small bars.

Peanut Butter and Jelly Bars

MAKES 12 BARS

- **3 cups all-purpose flour**
- **1 teaspoon salt**
- **1 teaspoon baking powder**
- **½ teaspoon baking soda**
- **1¼ cups packed dark brown sugar**
- **1 cup (2 sticks) unsalted butter, softened**
- **1 cup creamy peanut butter**
- **1 cup chunky peanut butter**
- **2 eggs**
- **2½ teaspoons vanilla**
- **1 cup raspberry jam**

1 Grease 8-inch square baking pan; line with parchment paper. Combine flour, salt, baking powder and baking soda in medium bowl.

2 Place brown sugar, butter and peanut butters in bowl of KitchenAid stand mixer. Attach bowl and flat beater to mixer. Turn to speed 2; mix 2 minutes or until well blended. With mixer running, add eggs and vanilla; beat until well blended. Scrape bottom and side of bowl. With mixer running on Stir speed, gradually add flour mixture, mixing just until combined.

3 Divide dough in half. Press half of dough into prepared pan. Wrap remaining dough in plastic wrap. Freeze dough and pan at least 2 hours.

4 Preheat oven to 350°F. Spread jam over dough in pan. Using large holes of box grater, grate frozen dough over jam. Bake 30 to 35 minutes or until edges begin to brown. Cool completely in pan on wire rack. Cut into bars.

Fudgy Brownies

MAKES 2 TO 3 DOZEN BROWNIES

1 cup (2 sticks) unsalted butter

8 ounces semisweet baking chocolate, coarsely chopped

1 cup sugar

4 eggs

1 teaspoon vanilla

1 teaspoon salt

1¼ cups all-purpose flour

2 cups dark or semisweet chocolate chips, divided

¼ cup heavy whipping cream

1 container (about 2 ounces) rainbow nonpareils

1 Preheat oven to 350°F. Grease 13×9-inch baking pan or line with parchment paper.

2 Melt butter and chocolate in large heavy saucepan over low heat; stir until melted and smooth. Transfer to bowl of KitchenAid stand mixer. Attach bowl and flat beater to mixer. Add sugar; turn to speed 2 and mix until blended. With mixer running, add eggs one at a time, beating until well blended after each addition. Scrape bottom and side of bowl. Add vanilla and salt; turn to Stir speed and mix until blended. Add flour and 1 cup chocolate chips; turn to Stir speed and mix just until blended. Spread batter evenly in prepared pan.

3 Bake 22 to 25 minutes or until center is set and toothpick inserted into center comes out clean. Cool completely in pan on wire rack.

4 Heat cream in small saucepan over medium-low heat until bubbles appear around edge of pan. Remove from heat; add remaining 1 cup chocolate chips. Let stand 1 minute; whisk until smooth and well blended. Spread evenly over brownies; top with nonpareils. Let stand at room temperature or refrigerate until topping is set. Cut into bars.

Caramel Chocolate Chunk Blondies

MAKES 2 TO 3 DOZEN BLONDIES

1½ **cups all-purpose flour**

1 **teaspoon baking powder**

1 **teaspoon salt**

¾ **cup granulated sugar**

¾ **cup packed brown sugar**

½ **cup (1 stick) unsalted butter, softened**

2 **eggs**

1½ **teaspoons vanilla**

1 **package (11½ ounces) semisweet chocolate chunks or 10 ounces chopped bittersweet chocolate**

5 **tablespoons caramel ice cream topping**

Flaky sea salt (optional)

1 Preheat oven to 350°F. Line 13×9-inch baking pan with parchment paper.

2 Combine flour, baking powder and 1 teaspoon salt in medium bowl. Combine granulated sugar, brown sugar and butter in bowl of KitchenAid stand mixer. Attach bowl and flat beater to mixer. Turn to speed 4; beat until smooth and creamy. Beat in eggs and vanilla until well blended. Scrape bottom and side of bowl. With mixer running on Stir speed, gradually beat in flour mixture until blended. Stir in chocolate chunks.

3 Spread batter evenly in prepared pan. Drop spoonfuls of caramel topping over batter; swirl into batter with knife. Sprinkle with sea salt, if desired.

4 Bake about 30 minutes or until edges are golden brown (center will be puffed and will not look set). Cool completely in pan on wire rack. Remove from pan using parchment; cut into bars.

Pies and Tarts

Mango Lime Galettes

MAKES 4 SERVINGS

PASTRY DOUGH

1⅔ **cups all-purpose flour**

2 **teaspoons granulated sugar**

¼ **teaspoon salt**

11 **tablespoons cold unsalted butter, cut into tablespoons**

6 **to 10 tablespoons ice water**

FILLING

1 **package (8 ounces) cream cheese, softened**

⅓ **cup granulated sugar**

1 **egg**

Grated peel and juice of 1 lime

TOPPING

2 **Ataulfo (Champagne) mangos or regular mangos, peeled and diced**

1 **egg**

¼ **cup water**

Sparkling decorating sugar

1 For pastry dough, place flour, 2 teaspoons granulated sugar and salt in bowl of KitchenAid stand mixer. Attach bowl and flat beater to mixer. With mixer running on speed 2, gradually add butter; mix about 2 minutes or until mixture resembles coarse crumbs. With mixer running, sprinkle in just enough ice water until dough begins to form. Press dough into a ball. Wrap dough in plastic wrap; refrigerate 30 minutes.

2 For filling, combine cream cheese, ⅓ cup granulated sugar, egg and grated lime peel and juice in clean mixer bowl. Attach bowl and flat beater to mixer. Turn to speed 4; mix until smooth and well blended. Transfer to small bowl; cover and refrigerate until ready to use.

3 Line baking sheet with parchment paper. Divide dough into four pieces. Roll out each piece on lightly floured surface into 6-inch circle, ¼ inch thick; place on prepared baking sheet. Spread one fourth of filling in center of each circle; fold and crimp edges of dough over filling. Top with mangos.

4 Whisk 1 egg and ¼ cup water in small bowl. Brush over edges of dough; sprinkle with sparkling sugar. Freeze galettes on baking sheet 20 minutes.

5 Preheat oven to 400°F. Bake galettes 20 to 25 minutes or until crust is golden brown and filling is bubbly, rotating pan once during baking.

Peanut Butter Pie

MAKES 12 SERVINGS

CRUST

- **2 cups graham cracker crumbs**
- **½ cup (1 stick) unsalted butter, melted**
- **¼ cup packed brown sugar**
- **2 tablespoons creamy peanut butter**
- **1 tablespoon chunky peanut butter**

FILLING

- **1 package (8 ounces) cream cheese, softened**
- **1½ cups powdered sugar, divided**
- **½ cup creamy peanut butter**
- **¼ cup chunky peanut butter**
- **2 cups heavy whipping cream**
- **¼ cup semisweet chocolate chips, melted**

1 For crust, preheat oven to 350°F. Place cracker crumbs, butter, brown sugar, 2 tablespoons creamy peanut butter and 1 tablespoon chunky peanut butter in bowl of KitchenAid stand mixer. Attach bowl and flat beater to mixer. Turn to speed 2; mix 1 minute or until mixture resembles wet sand. Press into 10-inch springform pan. Bake 10 minutes. Cool completely on wire rack.

2 For filling, place cream cheese, 1 cup powdered sugar, ½ cup creamy peanut butter and ¼ cup chunky peanut butter in clean mixer bowl. Attach bowl and flat beater to mixer. Turn to Stir speed; mix 1 minute or until well blended. Turn to speed 4; beat until creamy and completely smooth. Transfer to large bowl.

3 Pour cream into clean mixer bowl. Attach bowl and wire whip to mixer. Turn to Stir speed; add remaining ½ cup powdered sugar and mix until well blended. Turn to speed 8; whip until stiff peaks form. Gently fold whipped cream into peanut butter mixture with rubber spatula.

4 Spread filling into cooled crust. Freeze 3 to 4 hours or until firm. Drizzle with melted chocolate.

Raspberry Tart

MAKES 6 TO 8 SERVINGS

TART DOUGH

- 1¼ **cups plus 2 tablespoons all-purpose flour**
- ¼ **cup granulated sugar**
- ⅛ **teaspoon salt**
- ½ **cup (1 stick) cold unsalted butter, cut into cubes**
- 2 **tablespoons heavy whipping cream**
- 1 **egg yolk**

FILLING

- ¼ **cup (½ stick) unsalted butter**
- ¼ **vanilla bean, split lengthwise**
- 1 **egg, at room temperature**
- 5 **tablespoons granulated sugar**
- ¼ **cup all-purpose flour**
- ¼ **teaspoon salt**
- 2 **cups fresh raspberries**

  Powdered sugar

1 For dough, combine 1¼ cups plus 2 tablespoons flour, ¼ cup granulated sugar and ⅛ teaspoon salt in bowl of KitchenAid stand mixer. Attach bowl and flat beater to mixer. With mixer running on speed 2, gradually add butter; mix about 2 minutes or until mixture resembles coarse crumbs.

2 Whisk cream and egg yolk in small bowl until well blended. With mixer running, drizzle in cream mixture; mix 30 seconds to 1 minute or until dough forms. Turn out dough onto sheet of parchment paper; shape dough into a disc. Top with another piece of parchment paper. Roll out dough with rolling pin between parchment sheets into ¼-inch-thick rectangle slightly larger than 13×4-inch tart pan with removable bottom. Slide dough between parchment sheets onto baking sheet. Refrigerate at least 20 minutes or until cold.

3 Meanwhile for filling, melt ¼ cup butter in small saucepan over medium-low heat. Scrape seeds from vanilla bean; add seeds and pod to butter. Continue to cook until butter is brown and smells nutty, swirling pan frequently. Remove from heat; remove and discard vanilla bean pod. Pour butter into clean mixer bowl; let cool to room temperature.

4 Add egg. Turn mixer to speed 2; mix 1 minute or until blended. Add 5 tablespoons granulated sugar, ¼ cup flour and ¼ teaspoon salt; mix just until moistened. Scrape bottom and side of bowl; stir until completely blended.*

5 Lift off top sheet of parchment from dough; flip dough into 13×4-inch tart pan. Press dough evenly onto bottom and up sides of pan. Remove parchment; gently press any cracks back together with fingers. Roll the rolling pin across top of pan to trim excess dough. Prick bottom all over with fork. Line tart shell with parchment; freeze 20 minutes.**

6 Preheat oven to 400°F. Fill tart shell with pie weights or dried beans. Bake 12 minutes or until shell is set and light golden brown. Carefully remove parchment and pie weights; cool tart shell 10 minutes. *Reduce oven temperature to 350°F.* Spread filling evenly into tart shell. Arrange raspberries in even rows on top of filling.

7 Bake 35 to 40 minutes or until filling is golden brown and puffs around raspberries. Cool completely on wire rack. Remove side of pan. Dust with powdered sugar just before serving, if desired. The tart is best served the day it is baked.

*The filling can be made 1 day in advance; store, covered, in refrigerator and bring to room temperature before using.
**The tart shell can be frozen, well wrapped, at this point for up to 1 month. Bake as directed in step 6.

Chocolate Pecan Pie

MAKES 1 PIE

PIE PASTRY

- 1¼ **cups all-purpose flour**
- ½ **teaspoon salt**
- 3 **tablespoons shortening**
- 3 **tablespoons cold unsalted butter, cubed**
- 3 **to 4 tablespoons ice water**
- ½ **teaspoon cider vinegar**

FILLING

- 4 **eggs**
- 1 **cup sugar**
- 1 **cup dark corn syrup**
- 3 **ounces unsweetened chocolate, melted**
- 2 **cups pecan halves**

1 For pie pastry, combine flour and salt in bowl of KitchenAid stand mixer. Add shortening and butter. Turn to Stir speed; mix 1 to 2 minutes or until mixture resembles coarse crumbs. Combine 3 tablespoons ice water and vinegar in small bowl. With mixer running on Stir speed, drizzle in water mixture; mix just until dough begins to form, adding additional water if needed. Shape dough into a disc; wrap in plastic wrap. Refrigerate 30 minutes.

2 Preheat oven to 350°F. Roll out dough to ⅛-inch thickness between sheets of parchment paper. Fold pastry into quarters. Ease into 8- or 9-inch pie plate and unfold, pressing firmly against bottom and sides. Fold edge under. Crimp as desired. Refrigerate until ready to fill.

3 For filling, combine eggs, sugar and corn syrup in mixer bowl. Attach bowl and flat beater to mixer. Turn to speed 8; beat 1 minute. Scrape bottom and side of bowl.

4 Turn mixer to speed 6; gradually add chocolate and beat 1 minute or until well blended. Stir in pecans. Pour mixture into crust.

5 Bake 35 to 45 minutes or until top and crust are golden brown and center is slightly soft. Cool completely on wire rack.

Key Lime Pie

MAKES 8 SERVINGS

CRUST

- 12 whole graham crackers*
- ⅓ cup unsalted butter, melted
- 3 tablespoons sugar

FILLING

- 2 cans (14 ounces each) sweetened condensed milk
- ¾ cup key lime juice
- 6 egg yolks
- Pinch of salt
- Whipped cream** and fresh lime slices (optional)

*Or substitute 1½ cups graham cracker crumbs. In step 2, stir crumbs, butter and sugar in medium bowl until well blended.

**See page 5 for a recipe for sweetened whipped cream.*

1 Preheat oven to 350°F. Grease 9-inch pie plate or springform pan.

2 For crust, place graham crackers in food processor; pulse until fine crumbs form. Add butter and sugar; pulse until well blended. Press mixture onto bottom and 1 inch up side of prepared pie plate. Bake 8 minutes or until lightly browned. Cool on wire rack 10 minutes. *Reduce oven temperature to 325°F.*

3 For filling, place sweetened condensed milk, lime juice, egg yolks and salt in bowl of KitchenAid stand mixer. Attach bowl and flat beater to mixer. Turn mixer to speed 2; mix 1 minute or until well blended and smooth. Pour into crust.

4 Bake 20 minutes or until top is set. Cool completely in pan on wire rack. Cover and refrigerate 2 hours or overnight. Garnish with whipped cream and lime slices.

Cinnamon Apple Crostata

MAKES 8 TO 12 SERVINGS

PASTRY DOUGH

- 1½ cups all-purpose flour
- 3 tablespoons granulated sugar
- ½ teaspoon salt
- 10 tablespoons cold unsalted butter, cut into pieces
- 2 teaspoons vanilla
- 2 tablespoons ice water

TOPPING

- ½ cup all-purpose flour
- 5 tablespoons granulated sugar
- 3 tablespoons cold unsalted butter, cut into pieces
- 1 teaspoon ground cinnamon
- ¼ teaspoon salt

FILLING

- 2 large Honeycrisp apples, peeled, cored, quartered and sliced
- ¼ cup packed brown sugar
- 1 tablespoon fresh lemon juice
- ½ teaspoon ground cinnamon
- 1 egg, beaten

1 For pastry dough, place 1½ cups flour, 3 tablespoons granulated sugar and ½ teaspoon salt in bowl of KitchenAid stand mixer. Attach bowl and flat beater to mixer. With mixer running on Stir speed, gradually add 10 tablespoons butter; mix about 2 minutes or until mixture resembles coarse crumbs. With mixer running, sprinkle in vanilla and just enough ice water until dough begins to form. Shape dough into a disc; wrap with plastic wrap. Refrigerate 30 minutes.

2 For topping, place ½ cup flour, 5 tablespoons granulated sugar, 3 tablespoons butter, 1 teaspoon cinnamon and ¼ teaspoon salt in mixer bowl. Attach bowl and flat beater to mixer. Turn mixer to Stir speed; mix until coarse crumbs form. Transfer to small bowl; cover and refrigerate until ready to use.

3 For filling, combine apples, brown sugar, lemon juice and ½ teaspoon cinnamon in large bowl. Toss to coat. Let stand at room temperature 20 to 30 minutes.

4 Preheat oven to 400°F. Line baking sheet with parchment paper. Roll out dough to ¼-inch thickness on lightly floured surface. Shape ragged edges into smooth oval shape. Place dough on prepared baking sheet. Drain apples; spread apples in even layer over dough, leaving 1-inch border. Sprinkle topping evenly over apples; fold edge of dough over apples, pressing lightly to secure. Brush edge of dough with egg.

5 Bake 35 to 40 minutes or until lightly browned. Cool slightly; cut into wedges. Serve warm or at room temperature.

Cakes and Cupcakes

Vegan Chocolate Cake

MAKES 12 TO 16 SERVINGS

CAKE

- **6 tablespoons boiling water**
- **2 tablespoons ground flaxseed**
- **2 cups granulated sugar**
- **2 cups all-purpose flour**
- **1 cup unsweetened cocoa powder**
- **1 tablespoon instant espresso powder***
- **1½ teaspoons baking soda**
- **1½ teaspoons baking powder**
- **1½ teaspoons salt**
- **¾ cup plain unsweetened almond milk**
- **½ cup vegetable oil**
- **1 tablespoon apple cider vinegar**
- **2 teaspoons vanilla**
- **1 cup hot water***

FROSTING

- **1 package (12 ounces) vegan chocolate chips**
- **¼ teaspoon salt**
- **1 can (about 13 ounces) full-fat coconut milk**
- **2 cups powdered sugar**
- **Colored decors (optional)**

Or substitute 1 cup hot strong coffee for the espresso powder and hot water.

1 Preheat oven to 350°F. Grease 13×9-inch baking pan. Combine boiling water and flaxseed in small bowl; cool completely.

2 For cake, combine granulated sugar, flour, cocoa, espresso powder, baking soda, baking powder and 1½ teaspoons salt in bowl of KitchenAid stand mixer. Attach bowl and wire whip to mixer. Turn to Stir speed; mix until well blended.

3 Whisk almond milk, oil, vinegar, vanilla and flaxseed mixture in medium bowl until well blended. With mixer running on Stir speed, add to dry ingredients. Add hot water; mix until well blended. Pour into prepared pan.

4 Bake about 30 minutes or until top appears dry and toothpick inserted into center comes out clean. Cool completely in pan on wire rack.

5 For frosting, place chocolate chips and ¼ teaspoon salt in clean mixer bowl. Bring coconut milk to a simmer in small saucepan over medium heat, whisking frequently to blend. Pour 1 cup coconut milk over chips; swirl to coat. Let stand 5 minutes; whisk until smooth. Cool to room temperature.** Attach bowl and flat beater to mixer. Add powdered sugar to bowl. Turn to Stir speed; mix until blended. Increase to speed 8; beat 1 to 2 minutes or until frosting is fluffy and smooth. If frosting is too thick, add remaining coconut milk by teaspoonfuls until desired consistency is reached. Spread frosting over cake; sprinkle with decors, if desired.

**To frost cake with ganache instead of frosting, spread cooled mixture over top of cake at this point (skip the powdered sugar). For firm ganache, refrigerate until set.

Raspberry White Chocolate Cheesecake

MAKES 12 SERVINGS

CRUST

24 crème-filled chocolate sandwich cookies, crushed into fine crumbs

3 tablespoons unsalted butter, melted

FILLING

4 packages (8 ounces each) cream cheese, softened

1¼ cups sugar

½ cup sour cream

2 teaspoons vanilla

5 eggs, at room temperature

1 bar (4 ounces) white chocolate, chopped into ¼-inch pieces

⅔ cup seedless raspberry jam, stirred

Shaved white chocolate, whipped cream* and fresh raspberries

See page 5 for a recipe for sweetened whipped cream.

1 Preheat oven to 350°F. Grease 9-inch springform pan. Line bottom and side of pan with parchment paper. Wrap outside of pan tightly with foil.

2 For crust, combine crushed cookies and butter in small bowl; mix well. Press mixture onto bottom and 1 inch up side of prepared pan. Bake about 8 minutes or until firm. Cool completely on wire rack. *Increase oven temperature to 450°F.* Bring large pot of water to a boil.

3 For filling, place cream cheese in bowl of KitchenAid stand mixer. Attach bowl and flat beater to mixer. Turn to speed 2; mix until creamy. Add sugar, sour cream and vanilla; beat on speed 2 until smooth and well blended. Scrape bottom and side of bowl. With mixer running on speed 4, add eggs one at a time, beating until blended after each addition. Fold in chopped white chocolate with spatula. Spread one third of filling in crust. Drop half of jam by teaspoonfuls over filling; swirl gently with small knife or skewer, being careful not to overmix. Top with one third of filling; drop remaining jam by teaspoonfuls over filling and gently swirl jam. Spread remaining filling over top.

4 Place springform pan in large roasting pan; place in oven. Carefully add boiling water to come halfway up side of springform pan. *Immediately reduce oven temperature to 350°F.*

5 Bake about 1 hour 10 minutes or until top of cheesecake is lightly browned and center jiggles slightly. Remove cheesecake from roasting pan to wire rack; remove foil. Cool to room temperature. Cover and refrigerate 4 hours or overnight.

6 Remove side of pan; peel off parchment from side of cake. Garnish with shaved white chocolate, whipped cream and raspberries.

Boston Cream Cupcakes

MAKES 12 SERVINGS

FILLING

- **1 cup milk**
- **2 egg yolks**
- **1 whole egg**
- **¼ cup sugar**
- **1 teaspoon vanilla**
- **2 tablespoons cornstarch**

GANACHE

- **1 cup heavy whipping cream**
- **1 cup chopped semisweet chocolate**

CUPCAKES

- **2 eggs, separated**
- **½ cup plus 1 tablespoon sugar, divided**
- **1 cup sifted cake flour**
- **2 teaspoons baking powder**
- **¼ teaspoon salt**
- **½ cup milk**
- **4 tablespoons (½ stick) unsalted butter, melted**
- **1½ teaspoons vanilla**

1 For filling, heat 1 cup milk in small saucepan just until steaming. Remove from heat.

2 Whisk 2 egg yolks, 1 whole egg, ¼ cup sugar and 1 teaspoon vanilla in small bowl until well blended. Gradually whisk in hot milk in very thin steady stream. Whisk in cornstarch until well blended. Return to saucepan. Cook over medium-high heat 3 to 5 minutes or until custard thickens and starts to bubble, stirring constantly. Transfer to medium bowl; cover with plastic wrap, pressing directly onto surface of custard. Refrigerate until cold.

3 For ganache, heat cream in small saucepan just until bubbles appear around edge of pan. Place chocolate in small bowl; pour cream over chocolate. Let stand 1 minute. Whisk until smooth and shiny. Set aside.

4 For cupcakes, preheat oven to 350°F. Line 12 standard (2½-inch) muffin pan cups with paper baking cups.

5 Place egg whites in bowl of KitchenAid stand mixer. Attach bowl and wire whip to mixer. Turn to speed 10; whip until foamy. With mixer running, gradually add 1 tablespoon sugar; whip until stiff peaks form. Transfer to small bowl.

6 Place flour, remaining ½ cup sugar, baking powder and salt in mixer bowl. Attach bowl and flat beater to mixer. Turn to Stir speed; mix 1 minute or until combined.

7 Whisk ½ cup milk, butter, 2 egg yolks and 1½ teaspoons vanilla in another small bowl until blended. Add to flour mixture. Turn to speed 2; mix 1 minute or until blended. Gently fold egg whites into batter with spatula until blended. Scoop batter evenly into prepared muffin cups.

8 Bake 15 minutes or until golden brown and toothpick inserted into centers comes out clean. Remove to wire rack; cool completely.

9 Spoon cream filling into piping bag fitted with small round tip. Turn cupcakes over and stick tip into cupcakes through baking cups; pipe filling into cupcakes in two different spots until it reaches the top. Dip tops of cupcakes in ganache.

Decadent Chocolate Layer Cake

MAKES 8 TO 10 SERVINGS

CAKE

- 2½ **cups all-purpose flour**
- 2 **cups unsweetened cocoa powder**
- 2 **teaspoons salt**
- 2 **teaspoons baking powder**
- 1 **teaspoon baking soda**
- 3 **cups granulated sugar**
- ½ **cup (1 stick) unsalted butter, softened**
- ½ **cup vegetable oil**
- 4 **eggs**
- 2 **teaspoons vanilla**
- 1 **cup buttermilk**
- 1 **cup hot water**
- ¼ **cup maple syrup**

ESPRESSO FROSTING

- 1 **tablespoon instant espresso powder**
- 2 **tablespoons hot water**
- ¼ **cup heavy whipping cream**
- ¼ **cup milk**
- 2 **teaspoons vanilla**
- 5 **cups powdered sugar**
- 1½ **cups (3 sticks) unsalted butter, softened**
- 1½ **cups unsweetened cocoa powder**
- **Chocolate shavings (optional)**

1 Preheat oven to 350°F. Grease three 9-inch round cake pans; line bottoms with parchment paper.

2 For cake, whisk flour, 2 cups cocoa, salt, baking powder and baking soda in medium bowl. Combine granulated sugar, ½ cup butter and oil in bowl of KitchenAid stand mixer. Attach bowl and flat beater to mixer. Turn to speed 4; beat 5 minutes until mixture is white and fluffy. Add eggs one at a time, beating 30 seconds after each addition. Add 2 teaspoons vanilla; mix well. Scrape bottom and side of bowl.

3 With mixer running on Stir speed, alternately add buttermilk and flour mixture in three additions, mixing just until blended after each addition. Scrape bottom and side of bowl. With mixer running on Stir speed, add 1 cup hot water. Turn to speed 2; mix 1 minute. Pour into prepared pans.

4 Bake 18 to 22 minutes or until toothpick inserted into centers comes out clean. Turn out onto wire rack; remove parchment. Cool 30 minutes. Refrigerate 1 hour.

5 Meanwhile for espresso frosting, dissolve espresso powder in 2 tablespoons hot water in small bowl. Add cream, milk and 2 teaspoons vanilla. Combine powdered sugar, 1½ cups butter and 1½ cups cocoa in mixer bowl. Attach bowl and flat beater to mixer. Turn to Stir speed; mix 1 minute or until blended. Drizzle in cream mixture. Increase to speed 5; beat 1 minute. Increase to speed 8; beat 5 minutes or until very fluffy.

6 Place one cake layer on serving plate, bottom side up. Brush with some of maple syrup; spread with 1 cup frosting. Repeat with remaining cake layers, maple syrup and additional frosting; frost top and side of cake. Garnish with chocolate shavings, if desired.

Carrot Cake

MAKES 8 TO 10 SERVINGS

CAKE

- **2 cups all-purpose flour**
- **2 teaspoons baking soda**
- **2 teaspoons ground cinnamon**
- **1 teaspoon salt**
- **4 eggs**
- **2¼ cups granulated sugar**
- **1 cup vegetable oil**
- **1 cup buttermilk**
- **1 tablespoon vanilla**
- **3 medium carrots, shredded (3 cups)**
- **3 cups walnuts, chopped and toasted, divided**
- **1 cup shredded coconut**
- **1 can (8 ounces) crushed pineapple**

FROSTING

- **2 packages (8 ounces each) cream cheese, softened**
- **1 cup (2 sticks) unsalted butter, softened**
- **Pinch of salt**
- **3 cups powdered sugar**
- **1 tablespoon orange juice**
- **2 teaspoons grated orange peel**
- **1 teaspoon vanilla**

1 Preheat oven to 350°F. Grease two 9-inch round cake pans. Line bottoms with parchment paper; grease paper.

2 For cake, whisk flour, baking soda, cinnamon and 1 teaspoon salt in medium bowl. Place eggs in bowl of KitchenAid stand mixer. Attach bowl and wire whip to mixer. Turn to speed 4; whip until blended. Add granulated sugar, oil, buttermilk and 1 tablespoon vanilla; whip on speed 4 until well blended. Add flour mixture. Turn to Stir speed; mix until well blended. Stir in carrots, 1 cup walnuts, coconut and pineapple with spatula just until blended. Pour batter into prepared pans.

3 Bake 25 to 30 minutes or until toothpick inserted into centers comes out clean. Cool in pans 10 minutes. Turn out onto wire rack; remove parchment. Cool completely.

4 For frosting, combine cream cheese, butter and pinch of salt in mixer bowl. Attach bowl and flat beater to mixer. Turn to speed 5; beat 3 minutes or until creamy. Add powdered sugar, orange juice, orange peel and 1 teaspoon vanilla. Turn mixer to speed 2; beat until blended. Scrape bottom and side of bowl. Turn to speed 5; beat 2 minutes or until frosting is smooth.

5 Place one cake layer on serving plate; spread with 2 cups frosting. Top with second cake layer; frost top and side of cake with remaining frosting. Press 1¾ cups walnuts onto side of cake. Sprinkle remaining ¼ cup walnuts over top of cake.

Mixed Berry Almond Cake

MAKES 8 SERVINGS

CAKE

- **1 cup plus 3 tablespoons all-purpose flour**
- **⅓ cup almond flour**
- **¾ teaspoon baking powder**
- **¾ teaspoon salt**
- **½ cup (1 stick) plus 3 tablespoons unsalted butter, softened**
- **1 cup granulated sugar**
- **1 teaspoon vanilla bean paste or extract**
- **2 eggs**
- **¾ cup milk**
- **1½ cups frozen mixed berries**

FROSTING

- **4 ounces cream cheese, softened**
- **¼ cup powdered sugar**
- **1 teaspoon grated lemon peel**
- **½ cup heavy whipping cream**
- **Fresh berries for garnish (optional)**

1 Preheat oven to 350°F. Grease 8-inch round cake pan; line bottom with parchment paper. Combine all-purpose flour, almond flour, baking powder and salt in small bowl.

2 Place butter, granulated sugar and vanilla in bowl of KitchenAid stand mixer. Attach bowl and flat beater to mixer. Turn to speed 6; beat 3 minutes or until light and fluffy. Scrape bottom and side of bowl. Turn to speed 4; add eggs one at a time, beating well after each addition. Scrape bottom and side of bowl.

3 With mixer running on Stir speed, add flour mixture alternately with milk, beginning and ending with flour mixture. Gently fold in frozen berries; do not overmix. Pour batter into prepared pan.

4 Bake 35 to 40 minutes or until toothpick inserted into center comes out clean. Cool in pan on wire rack 10 minutes. Turn out onto wire rack; remove parchment. Cool completely.

5 For frosting, place cream cheese, powdered sugar and lemon peel in mixer bowl. Attach bowl and flat beater to mixer. Turn mixer to speed 4; beat until light and fluffy. Scrape bottom and side of bowl. With mixer running on Stir speed, drizzle in cream. Turn to speed 4; beat 1 minute or until thickened and spreadable. Spread over top of cake. Garnish with fresh berries.

Pumpkin Cheesecake

MAKES 12 SERVINGS

CRUST

18 graham crackers (2 sleeves)

¼ cup sugar

⅛ teaspoon salt

½ cup (1 stick) unsalted butter, melted

FILLING

1 can (15 ounces) pumpkin purée

¼ cup sour cream

2 teaspoons vanilla

2 teaspoons ground cinnamon

1 teaspoon ground ginger

¼ teaspoon salt

¼ teaspoon ground cloves

4 packages (8 ounces each) cream cheese, softened

1¾ cups sugar

5 eggs

Whipped cream*

*See page 5 for a recipe for sweetened whipped cream.

1 Grease 9-inch springform pan. Line bottom with parchment paper. Wrap outside of pan tightly with foil.

2 For crust, place graham crackers in food processor; pulse until fine crumbs form. Add ¼ cup sugar and ⅛ teaspoon salt; pulse to blend. Add butter; pulse until crumbs are moistened and mixture is well blended. Press onto bottom and all the way up side of prepared pan in thin layer. Refrigerate at least 20 minutes. Preheat oven to 350°F.

3 Bake crust 12 minutes. Cool on wire rack. Bring large pot of water to a boil.

4 For filling, whisk pumpkin, sour cream, vanilla, cinnamon, ginger, ¼ teaspoon salt and cloves in medium bowl until well blended. Place cream cheese and 1¾ cups sugar in bowl of KitchenAid stand mixer. Attach bowl and flat beater to mixer. Turn to speed 4; beat 1 minute or until smooth. With mixer running, add eggs one at a time, beating until blended after each addition. Scrape bottom and side of bowl. Add pumpkin mixture. Turn mixer to speed 5; beat until well blended. Pour into crust; smooth top.

5 Place springform pan in large roasting pan; place in oven. Carefully add boiling water to roasting pan to come about halfway up side of springform pan.

6 Bake 1 hour 10 minutes or until top is set and lightly browned but still jiggly. Remove cheesecake from roasting pan to wire rack; remove foil. Cool to room temperature.

7 Run small thin spatula around edge of pan to loosen crust. (Do not remove side of pan.) Cover with plastic wrap; refrigerate 8 hours or overnight. Remove side of pan. Garnish with whipped cream.

Cookies and Cream Sheet Cake

MAKES 24 SERVINGS

CAKE

- **3 egg whites**
- **1⅔ cups granulated sugar, divided**
- **2¼ cups all-purpose flour**
- **2 teaspoons baking powder**
- **1 teaspoon baking soda**
- **¼ teaspoon salt**
- **1 cup milk**
- **½ cup (1 stick) unsalted butter, softened**
- **½ cup vegetable oil**
- **2 teaspoons vanilla**
- **2 cups coarsely crushed crème-filled chocolate sandwich cookies, plus additional for garnish**

FROSTING

- **¾ cup (1½ sticks) unsalted butter, softened**
- **2 cups powdered sugar**
- **1 tablespoon milk**
- **1 teaspoon vanilla**
- **1 jar (about 7 ounces) marshmallow crème**

1 Preheat oven to 350°F. Line 13×9-inch baking pan with parchment paper.

2 Place egg whites in bowl of KitchenAid stand mixer. Attach bowl and wire whip to mixer. Turn to speed 10; whip until frothy. With mixer running, add ⅓ cup granulated sugar in steady stream. Continue to whip 1 minute or until stiff, glossy peaks form. Transfer eggs whites to small bowl.

3 Combine flour, remaining 1⅓ cups granulated sugar, baking powder, baking soda and salt in mixer bowl. Attach bowl and flat beater to mixer. Turn to Stir speed; mix until blended. With mixer running, add 1 cup milk, ½ cup butter, oil and 2 teaspoons vanilla; mix just until blended. Increase to speed 5; beat 2 minutes.

4 Stir in one third of eggs whites with spatula until well blended. Gently fold in remaining egg whites until blended and no streaks of white remain. Fold in 2 cups crushed cookies. Pour into prepared pan; smooth top.

5 Bake 30 to 35 minutes or until top springs back when lightly touched and toothpick inserted into center comes out with a few moist crumbs attached. Cool completely in pan on wire rack.

6 For frosting, place ¾ cup butter, powdered sugar, 1 tablespoon milk and 1 teaspoon vanilla in mixer bowl. Attach bowl and flat beater to mixer. Turn to speed 8; beat 5 minutes or until very fluffy. Add marshmallow crème; beat until well blended. Spread over cake; garnish with additional crushed sandwich cookies.

Red Velvet Cake

MAKES 8 TO 10 SERVINGS

CAKE

- **2 cups all-purpose flour**
- **2 tablespoons unsweetened cocoa powder**
- **1 teaspoon salt**
- **1¼ cups buttermilk**
- **1 bottle (1 ounce) red food coloring**
- **1 teaspoon vanilla**
- **1½ cups granulated sugar**
- **1 cup (2 sticks) unsalted butter, softened**
- **2 eggs**
- **1 tablespoon white or cider vinegar**
- **1½ teaspoons baking soda**

FROSTING

- **2 packages (8 ounces each) cream cheese, softened**
- **½ cup (1 stick) unsalted butter, softened**
- **6 cups powdered sugar**
- **¼ cup milk**
- **2 teaspoons vanilla**
- **4 ounces white chocolate, shaved with vegetable peeler**

1 Preheat oven to 350°F. Grease three 9-inch round cake pans. Line bottoms with parchment paper; grease paper.

2 For cake, combine flour, cocoa and salt in medium bowl. Combine buttermilk, food coloring and vanilla in 2-cup glass measure; mix well.

3 Place granulated sugar and 1 cup butter in bowl of KitchenAid stand mixer. Attach bowl and flat beater to mixer. Turn to speed 6; beat 5 minutes or until light and fluffy. With mixer running, add eggs one at a time, beating until well blended after each addition. Scrape bottom and side of bowl. Turn to speed 2; add flour mixture alternately with buttermilk mixture, beating until blended after each addition. Stir vinegar into baking soda in small bowl. Add to batter; stir gently with spatula until blended. Pour batter into prepared pans.

4 Bake about 20 minutes or until toothpick inserted into centers comes out clean. Cool in pans 10 minutes. Turn out onto wire rack; remove parchment. Cool completely.

5 For frosting, place cream cheese and ½ cup butter in mixer bowl. Attach bowl and flat beater to mixer. Turn to speed 5; beat until creamy. Add powdered sugar, milk and 2 teaspoons vanilla; turn to speed 2 and beat until blended. Increase to speed 5; beat until smooth.

6 Place one cake layer on serving plate; spread with 1½ cups frosting. Top with second cake layer; spread with 1½ cups frosting. Top with remaining cake layer; spread remaining frosting over top and side of cake. Press white chocolate shavings onto side of cake.

Six-Layer Chocolate Cake

MAKES 12 SERVINGS

CAKE

4 cups all-purpose flour

4 cups sugar

1½ cups unsweetened cocoa powder

3½ teaspoons baking soda

1 tablespoon baking powder

2 teaspoons salt

4 eggs

2 cups buttermilk

1 cup vegetable or canola oil

4 teaspoons vanilla

2 cups very hot coffee

¾ cups semisweet chocolate chips

GANACHE

3 cups heavy whipping cream

¼ cup light corn syrup

⅛ teaspoon salt

6 cups semisweet chocolate chips

2 cups chopped walnuts

1 Preheat oven to 350°F. Grease three 9-inch round cake pans. Line bottoms with parchment paper; grease paper. Dust bottoms and sides of pans with flour.

2 For cake, combine flour, sugar, cocoa, baking soda, baking powder and 2 teaspoons salt in bowl of KitchenAid stand mixer. Attach bowl and flat beater to mixer. Turn to speed 2; mix until well blended.

3 Whisk eggs in medium bowl. Add buttermilk, oil and vanilla; whisk until well blended. With mixer running on speed 2, gradually add egg mixture to flour mixture (mixer will be very full), beating until blended. Increase to speed 5; beat 2 minutes. Scrape bottom and side of bowl. Turn to Stir speed; gradually add coffee, mixing until blended. (Batter will be thin.) Pour batter into prepared pans. Sprinkle each layer with ¼ cup chocolate chips.

4 Bake about 45 minutes or until toothpick inserted into centers comes out clean. (Rotate cake pans from top to bottom and left to right halfway through baking.) Cool in pans 10 minutes. Invert onto wire rack; remove parchment. Cool completely.

5 For ganache, combine cream, corn syrup and ⅛ teaspoon salt in large heavy saucepan. Heat over medium heat until bubbles appear around edge of pan. Remove from heat. Add 6 cups chocolate chips; let stand 3 minutes. Whisk until well blended and smooth. For filling, remove half of ganache (about 4 cups) to medium bowl; refrigerate 30 minutes to 1 hour or until thick and spreadable. Leave remaining ganache at room temperature.

6 Cut each cake layer in half horizontally with long serrated knife. Place one bottom cake layer, cut side up, on serving plate; spread with chilled filling (about ⅔ cup per layer). Top with second top cake layer, cut side up; spread with filling. Repeat with remaining cake layers and chilled filling until final cake layer is reached; place top layer cut side down over filling.

7 Microwave remaining ganache on LOW (30%) 2 to 3 minutes or just until pourable, stirring after each minute. Pour frosting over top of cake so it runs down side; use long metal spatula to smooth frosting around side of cake. Refrigerate 10 minutes or until frosting is partially set. Press walnuts onto side of cake.

Chocolate Cream Sandwich Cookie Cheesecake

MAKES 12 SERVINGS

CRUST

1½ **cups finely ground chocolate crème-filled sandwich cookies (about 16 cookies)**

6 **tablespoons unsalted butter, melted**

¼ **cup sugar**

FILLING

4 **packages (8 ounces each) cream cheese, softened**

¾ **cup sugar**

4 **eggs**

2 **teaspoons vanilla**

1 **cup white chocolate chips, melted and cooled slightly**

1 Preheat oven to 350°F. Grease 9-inch springform pan. Line bottom with parchment paper. Wrap outside of pan tightly with foil.

2 For crust, combine cookie crumbs, butter and sugar in medium bowl; stir until crumbs are moistened and mixture is well blended. Press evenly onto bottom of prepared pan. Bake 10 minutes. Cool on wire rack. Bring large pot of water to a boil.

3 For filling, place cream cheese and ¾ cup sugar in bowl of KitchenAid stand mixer. Attach bowl and flat beater to mixer. Turn to speed 4; beat 1 minute or until smooth. Scrape bottom and side of bowl. With mixer running on speed 4, add eggs one at a time, beating until well blended after each addition. Beat in vanilla. Scrape bottom and side of bowl.

4 Stir white chocolate and 1 cup cream cheese mixture in medium bowl until well blended. Add white chocolate mixture to remaining cream cheese mixture in mixer bowl. Turn to speed 4; beat until well blended. Pour into crust; smooth top. Place springform pan in large roasting pan; place in oven. Carefully add boiling water to roasting pan to come about halfway up side of springform pan.

5 Bake about 45 minutes or until top of cheesecake is lightly browned and center jiggles slightly. Remove cheesecake from roasting pan to wire rack; remove foil. Run small thin spatula around edge of pan to loosen crust. (Do not remove side of pan.) Cool to room temperature. Cover with plastic wrap; refrigerate 8 hours or overnight. Remove side of pan.

Sponge Cake with Passionfruit Topping

MAKES 8 SERVINGS

CAKE

- **1 cup all-purpose flour**
- **½ teaspoon baking powder**
- **½ teaspoon salt**
- **4 eggs, at room temperature**
- **⅔ cup granulated sugar**
- **3 tablespoons unsalted butter, melted**
- **½ teaspoon vanilla**

FILLING

- **1 cup heavy whipping cream**
- **3 tablespoons powdered sugar**
- **1½ teaspoons vanilla**

TOPPING

- **1 tablespoon unsalted butter**
- **2 tablespoons passionfruit purée or orange juice**
- **1 cup powdered sugar**

1 Preheat oven to 350°F. Grease and flour two 8-inch round cake pans. Sift flour and baking powder into small bowl; whisk in salt.

2 Place eggs and granulated sugar in bowl of KitchenAid stand mixer. Attach bowl and wire whip to mixer. Turn to speed 6; whip 10 minutes until very light and tripled in volume. Sprinkle half of flour over egg mixture; fold gently to mix. Repeat with remaining flour. Gently fold in melted butter and ½ teaspoon vanilla. Pour batter into prepared pans.

3 Bake 15 to 20 minutes or until tops are golden brown and toothpick inserted into centers comes out clean. Cool in pans 5 minutes. Turn out onto wire rack; cool completely.

4 For filling, place cream, 3 tablespoons powdered sugar and 1½ teaspoons vanilla in mixer bowl. Attach bowl and wire whip to mixer. Turn to speed 8; whip about 2 minutes or until soft peaks form. Refrigerate until needed.

5 Place one cake layer on serving plate; top with filling. Top with remaining cake layer.

6 For topping, melt 1 tablespoon butter in small saucepan; stir in passionfruit purée. Add 1 cup powdered sugar; whisk until well blended. Pour over top of cake. Serve immediately.

Desserts

Chocolate Mousse

MAKES 12 SERVINGS

1 cup heavy whipping cream

5 eggs, separated

⅓ cup strong brewed coffee or espresso, at room temperature

¼ cup plus 1 tablespoon superfine sugar, divided

½ teaspoon salt

5 ounces bittersweet chocolate, chopped

Shaved chocolate and/or whipped cream* (optional)

*See page 5 for a recipe for sweetened whipped cream.

1 Pour cream into bowl of KitchenAid stand mixer. Attach bowl and wire whip to mixer. Turn to speed 4, increasing to speed 8; whip 1 to 2 minutes or until soft peaks form. Transfer whipped cream to medium bowl. Cover and refrigerate until ready to use.

2 Place egg yolks, coffee, ¼ cup sugar and salt in clean mixer bowl. Attach bowl and wire whip to mixer. Turn to speed 6; mix 1 to 2 minutes or until light in color. Remove bowl from stand mixer and set over saucepan of simmering water, keeping bowl above water as much as possible. Cook 1 minute or until doubled in volume, whisking constantly. Remove bowl from heat; stir in chocolate until melted. Transfer mixture to large bowl and let cool to room temperature, whisking occasionally.

3 Place egg whites in clean mixer bowl. Attach bowl and wire whip to mixer. Turn to speed 8; whip 1 to 2 minutes or until foamy. Gradually add remaining 1 tablespoon sugar; whip until soft peaks form.

4 Fold egg whites into chocolate mixture with spatula in two additions. Gently fold in whipped cream just until blended. Divide mousse among 12 (4-ounce) ramekins. Refrigerate at least 2 hours or until firm. Serve with shaved chocolate or additional whipped cream, if desired.

Apple Clafoutis

MAKES 10 SERVINGS

- 9 **tablespoons unsalted butter, softened, divided**
- 1 **cup heavy whipping cream**
- 3 **eggs**
- ⅔ **cup all-purpose flour**
- 1 **cup sugar, divided**
- 1 **teaspoon vanilla**
- ½ **teaspoon salt**
- 3 **medium tart apples**
- 1 **teaspoon fresh lemon juice**
- 3 **tablespoons brandy**
- ½ **teaspoon ground cinnamon**

1 Preheat oven to 400°F. Grease 9-inch round or square baking dish with 1 tablespoon butter. Place prepared baking dish in oven to preheat 10 minutes before ready to bake.

2 Combine cream, eggs, 6 tablespoons butter, flour, ½ cup sugar, vanilla and salt in bowl of KitchenAid stand mixer. Attach bowl and flat beater to mixer. Turn to speed 2; mix about 30 seconds or until combined.

3 Remove flat beater; attach KitchenAid spiralizer to stand mixer. Center one apple on fruit and vegetable spike; attach to spiralizer. Attach peeler blade and medium core spiral slice blade and position at end of apple. Turn mixer to speed 3 and process until blade reaches end of apple. Repeat with remaining apples. Stand apples on end on cutting board; cut into half circles. Place in medium bowl. Add lemon juice; toss to coat.

4 Melt remaining 2 tablespoons butter in medium skillet over medium-high heat. Add apples and remaining ½ cup sugar; sauté 2 minutes. Add brandy; sauté 2 minutes. Transfer apples to medium bowl with slotted spoon, leaving juices in skillet.

5 Pour half of batter into hot baking dish. Arrange apples over batter; top with remaining batter and sprinkle with cinnamon.

6 Bake 18 to 20 minutes or until edge is golden and center is set. Let cool slightly. If desired, warm pan juices in skillet and drizzle over clafoutis.

Lemon Cream Dessert

MAKES 9 TO 12 SERVINGS

CAKE

- 1¾ cups all-purpose flour
- 1¼ teaspoons baking powder
- ½ teaspoon salt
- 4 eggs, separated
- 1½ cups granulated sugar
- ¾ cup (1½ sticks) unsalted butter, softened
- Grated peel of 2 lemons
- ¼ cup fresh lemon juice

LEMON CURD

- 1 cup granulated sugar
- ¾ cup (1½ sticks) unsalted butter
- ⅔ cup fresh lemon juice
- Grated peel of 2 lemons
- ¼ teaspoon salt
- 5 eggs, beaten
- ¼ cup heavy whipping cream

TOPPING

- 1 package (8 ounces) cream cheese, softened
- 1½ cups powdered sugar
- Lemon peel strips (optional)

1 Preheat oven to 350°F. Grease 9-inch square baking pan.

2 For cake, whisk flour, baking powder and ½ teaspoon salt in medium bowl. Place 4 egg whites in bowl of KitchenAid stand mixer. Attach bowl and wire whip to mixer. Turn to speed 10; whip until stiff peaks form. Transfer to small bowl.

3 Place 1½ cups granulated sugar and ¾ cup butter in mixer bowl. Attach bowl and flat beater to mixer. Turn to speed 6; beat 3 to 5 minutes or until light and fluffy. With mixer running on speed 5, add 4 egg yolks one at a time, beating well after each addition. Scrape bottom and side of bowl. Add grated peel of 2 lemons and ¼ cup lemon juice. Turn to Stir speed; beat until well blended. With mixer running, gradually add flour mixture just until blended. Gently stir in half of egg whites with spatula. Fold in remaining egg whites until no streaks of white remain. Spread batter in prepared pan.

4 Bake 35 to 38 minutes or until toothpick inserted into center comes out clean. Cool in pan on wire rack 10 minutes.

5 Meanwhile for lemon curd, combine 1 cup granulated sugar, ¾ cup butter, ⅔ cup lemon juice, grated peel of 2 lemons and ¼ teaspoon salt in medium saucepan; cook over medium heat until butter is melted and sugar is dissolved, stirring frequently. Gradually whisk in beaten eggs in thin steady stream. Cook over medium-low heat 5 minutes or until thickened to consistency of pudding, whisking constantly. Strain through fine-mesh sieve into medium bowl. Place ½ cup lemon curd in small bowl; press plastic wrap onto surface of remaining lemon curd in medium bowl. Cool to room temperature. Refrigerate until cold and thickened.

6 Stir cream into reserved ½ cup lemon curd. Poke holes all over warm cake with skewer. Spread cream mixture all over cake and press mixture into holes. Cover and refrigerate 1 hour.

7 For topping, place cream cheese in mixer bowl. Attach bowl and flat beater to mixer. Turn to speed 4; beat 1 minute or until creamy. Add powdered sugar and 1 cup lemon curd. Turn to speed 6; beat 2 minutes or until well blended and fluffy. Spread remaining lemon curd over top of cake; spread topping over lemon curd. Refrigerate 2 hours or overnight. Garnish with lemon peel strips.

Warm Chocolate Soufflé Cakes

MAKES 4 SERVINGS

6 tablespoons (¾ stick) unsalted butter

4 ounces semisweet chocolate, chopped

½ cup granulated sugar

1½ tablespoons cornstarch

⅛ teaspoon salt

2 eggs

2 egg yolks

Raspberry Sauce (recipe follows, optional)

Powdered sugar

1 Grease four 6-ounce ramekins. Place on small baking sheet.

2 Combine butter and chocolate in small saucepan; heat over low heat until mixture is melted and smooth, stirring frequently. Combine granulated sugar, cornstarch and salt in bowl of KitchenAid stand mixer. Attach bowl and wire whip to mixer. Turn to speed 2; mix until well blended. Add chocolate mixture to sugar mixture. Turn to speed 4; whip until well blended.

3 Add eggs and egg yolks to sugar mixture. Turn to speed 4; whip just until blended. Divide evenly among prepared ramekins; cover and refrigerate overnight. Prepare raspberry sauce, if desired.

4 Preheat oven to 375°F. Bake 18 to 20 minutes or just until cakes are barely set (batter does not jiggle or look shiny). Sprinkle with powdered sugar; serve with raspberry sauce, if desired.

Raspberry Sauce: Combine 1 (12-ounce) package thawed frozen raspberries and ¼ cup granulated sugar in food processor; process until smooth. Press through fine-mesh sieve to remove seeds. Refrigerate until ready to use.

Éclair Cake

MAKES 12 SERVINGS

CAKE

1 cup water

½ cup (1 stick) unsalted butter

1 cup all-purpose flour

¼ teaspoon salt

4 eggs

MOUSSE

1 cup heavy whipping cream

1¼ cups powdered sugar, divided

1 container (16 ounces) mascarpone cheese

3 teaspoons unsweetened cocoa powder, divided

1 teaspoon instant coffee granules

1 teaspoon coffee liqueur

½ teaspoon vanilla

1 Preheat oven to 400°F. Line baking sheet with parchment paper.

2 For cake, heat water and butter in small saucepan over medium heat until butter is melted. Transfer to bowl of KitchenAid stand mixer. Attach bowl and flat beater to mixer. Turn to speed 2. Gradually add flour and salt; mix 1 minute or until combined. With mixer running on speed 2, add eggs one at a time, mixing until well blended after each addition.

3 Spoon dough into large piping bag fitted with ¼-inch plain tip. Pipe long vertical strips of dough onto prepared baking sheet ¼ inch apart. Bake 20 minutes. Cool completely.

4 For mousse, place cream in clean mixer bowl. Attach bowl and wire whip to mixer. Turn to Stir speed; gradually add ½ cup powdered sugar. Turn to speed 8; whip until stiff peaks form. Transfer to medium bowl.

5 Place mascarpone, ½ cup powdered sugar, 2 teaspoons cocoa, coffee granules, liqueur and vanilla in mixer bowl. Attach bowl and flat beater to mixer. Turn to Stir speed; mix 1 minute or until well blended. Turn to speed 4; beat until light and fluffy. Gently fold whipped cream into mascarpone mixture with spatula.

6 Cut cake layer lengthwise into two squares using serrated knife. Spread mousse evenly onto one layer. Gently top with second cake layer.

7 Combine remaining ¼ cup powdered sugar and 1 teaspoon cocoa in small bowl. Sift over cake.

Pumpkin Ice Cream with Pistachio Brittle

MAKES 1½ QUARTS

- ¾ **cup canned pumpkin purée**
- ½ **cup packed brown sugar**
- ¼ **cup granulated sugar**
- 2 **teaspoons ground cinnamon**
- 1 **teaspoon ground ginger**
- ¼ **teaspoon salt**
- 1½ **cups heavy whipping cream**
- 1 **cup whole milk**
- 1 **tablespoon molasses**
- 4 **egg yolks**
- 1 **tablespoon cornstarch mixed with 1 tablespoon cold milk**

  Pistachio Brittle (page 97)

1 Cook pumpkin in medium saucepan over medium heat 5 minutes, stirring frequently. Add brown sugar, granulated sugar, cinnamon, ginger and salt; cook and stir 1 minute. Whisk in cream, milk and molasses; bring to a boil over medium-high heat, stirring frequently. Remove from heat.

2 Whisk egg yolks in small bowl. Slowly whisk in ½ cup hot pumpkin mixture in thin steady stream until blended. Slowly whisk egg yolk mixture back into saucepan in thin steady stream. Cook over medium heat 2 minutes or until mixture is thick enough to coat back of spoon. Add cornstarch mixture; cook and stir 1 minute.

3 Set fine-mesh strainer over medium bowl. Strain pumpkin mixture through strainer into bowl, pressing with spatula to force mixture through. Fill large bowl half full with cold water and ice. Place bowl with pumpkin mixture in ice bath; stir occasionally until mixture is cool.

4 Remove bowl from ice bath. Cover and refrigerate at least 4 hours or overnight. Attach KitchenAid ice cream maker bowl and dasher to stand mixer. Turn mixer to Stir speed; pour in ice cream mixture. Churn 20 to 25 minutes or until ice cream is the consistency of soft serve. Pack into freezer container and freeze until firm.

5 Prepare pistachio brittle. Break into small pieces; serve over ice cream.

Pistachio Brittle

1 cup granulated sugar

½ cup water

¼ cup corn syrup

¼ cup molasses

¼ teaspoon salt

⅛ teaspoon cream of tartar

1 cup roasted salted pistachio nuts

1 tablespoon butter, cut into pieces

¼ teaspoon baking soda

Flaky sea salt

1 Grease large baking sheet. Combine granulated sugar, water, corn syrup, molasses, ¼ teaspoon salt and cream of tartar in medium heavy saucepan; bring to a boil over medium-high heat, stirring once to blend. Clip candy thermometer to side of pan. Cook without stirring until mixture reaches 240°F. Add pistachios; cook until 295°F, stirring frequently.

2 Remove from heat; stir in butter and baking soda. Immediately spread mixture in thin layer on prepared baking sheet; sprinkle with flaky salt. Let stand until cool; break into pieces.

Yeast Breads

Braided Challah Bread

MAKES 1 LOAF

- 1 **cup warm water (105° to 110°F)**
- 1 **cup warm milk (105° to 110°F)**
- 1 **tablespoon active dry yeast**
- 2 **teaspoons sugar**
- 6 **cups all-purpose flour**
- 2 **tablespoons grated orange peel**
- 1 **tablespoon salt**
- 1 **can (12 ounces) evaporated milk**
- 2 **egg yolks**
- 1 **tablespoon salted butter, melted**
- 1 **whole egg**
- 2 **tablespoons water**

1 Combine warm water, milk, yeast and sugar in medium bowl; stir until yeast is dissolved. Let stand 10 minutes or until foamy.

2 Place flour, orange peel and salt in bowl of KitchenAid stand mixer. Attach bowl and flat beater to mixer. Turn to Stir speed; mix 1 minute or until blended. Add yeast mixture, evaporated milk, egg yolks and butter. Turn to speed 3; mix just until incorporated.

3 Replace flat beater with dough hook. Turn to speed 2; knead 7 minutes. Place dough in large lightly greased bowl; turn to grease top. Cover and let rise in warm place 2 hours or until doubled in size.

4 Grease baking sheet. Turn out dough onto lightly floured surface. Pat into rectangle; cut into three equal pieces. Roll each dough piece into long rope. Arrange dough ropes side by side; pinch ropes together at top. Pick up center rope and cross it over the rope on the right. Pick up left rope and cross it all the way over the rope on the right. Continue braiding; pinch bottom ends together. Place loaf on prepared baking sheet. Let rise in warm place 40 minutes or until doubled in size.

5 Preheat oven to 350°F. Whisk egg and 2 tablespoons water in small bowl; brush some of egg wash over loaf.

6 Bake 30 minutes or until lightly browned. Remove from oven and brush again with egg wash. Bake 10 minutes or until golden brown. Remove to wire rack; cool completely before slicing.

Pumpernickel Bread

MAKES 2 LOAVES

Vegetable oil for greasing pans

5 cups dark rye flour

2 cups plus 2 tablespoons all-purpose flour

¼ cup Dutch process cocoa powder

1 tablespoon active dry yeast

2½ teaspoons sugar

1½ teaspoons salt

2 cups (1 pint) dry hard apple cider, at room temperature

1 cup warm water (105° to 110°F)

3 tablespoons unsulphured blackstrap molasses

Olive oil for brushing

2 teaspoons fennel seeds

2 teaspoons caraway seeds

1 Grease two 9×5-inch loaf pans with vegetable oil.

2 Combine rye flour, all-purpose flour, cocoa, yeast, sugar and salt in bowl of KitchenAid stand mixer. Attach bowl and dough hook to mixer. Turn mixer to Stir speed; mix 1 minute until well blended. With mixer running, gradually add cider, water and molasses; mix until ingredients are moistened. Increase to speed 2; knead 10 minutes or until dough looks stringy and sticky.

3 Turn out dough onto lightly floured surface; sprinkle top of dough lightly with additional all-purpose flour. Cut dough in half with bench scraper or sharp knife. Shape each half into oblong loaf; place in prepared pans. Brush tops of loaves with olive oil; sprinkle with fennel and caraway seeds. Using very sharp paring knife, make three diagonal slashes ¼-inch deep on top of each loaf. Cover with plastic wrap; let rise in warm place about 1 hour or until dough reaches tops of pans.

4 Preheat oven to 400°F. Bake 35 to 40 minutes or until instant-read thermometer inserted into centers reads 200°F and loaves sound hollow when tapped. Remove to wire rack; cool completely before slicing.

Cheesy Stuffed Garlic-Butter Crescents

MAKES 8 SERVINGS

½ **cup warm milk (105° to 110°F)**

1 **tablespoon water**

1¼ **teaspoons active dry yeast**

2 **cups all-purpose flour**

1 **egg**

2¼ **teaspoons sugar**

¾ **teaspoon kosher salt**

3 **tablespoons unsalted butter, softened, divided**

2 **tablespoons roasted garlic purée**

2 **cups (8 ounces) shredded mozzarella cheese**

1 **tablespoon unsalted butter, melted**

¼ **teaspoon flaky sea salt**

1 Whisk milk, water and yeast in bowl of KitchenAid stand mixer until yeast is dissolved. Add flour, egg, sugar and kosher salt. Attach bowl and dough hook to mixer. Turn to Stir speed; mix 1 minute or until well blended. Add 2 tablespoons softened butter. Turn to speed 2; knead 3 to 4 minutes or until dough is smooth and elastic. Place dough in large lightly greased bowl; turn to grease top. Cover and let rise in warm place 40 minutes or until doubled in size.

2 Preheat oven to 400°F. Line baking sheet with parchment paper. Mix remaining 1 tablespoon softened butter and garlic purée in small bowl.

3 Turn out dough onto lightly floured surface; shape into a ball. Roll out into 16-inch circle with lightly floured rolling pin. Spread garlic butter over dough; sprinkle evenly with cheese. Cut dough into 16 triangles using pizza cutter. Roll up each triangle from wide edge to create crescent shape. Place on prepared baking sheet. Let stand in warm place 20 minutes.

4 Brush crescents with melted butter and sprinkle with sea salt. Bake 15 to 18 minutes or until puffed and golden brown. Cool slightly before serving.

Naan Bread with Harissa Yogurt

MAKES 4 SERVINGS

NAAN

- **2 cups all-purpose flour**
- **1 teaspoon sugar**
- **1 teaspoon active dry yeast**
- **1 teaspoon kosher salt**
- **5 tablespoons warm water (105° to 110°F)**
- **½ cup plain yogurt, at room temperature**
- **5 tablespoons vegetable oil, divided**
- **4 tablespoons ghee or clarified butter, melted**
- **⅛ teaspoon fine sea salt**

HARISSA YOGURT

- **1 cup plain yogurt**
- **2 tablespoons chopped fresh cilantro**
- **1¼ teaspoons harissa**
- **½ teaspoon kosher salt**
- **¼ teaspoon ground cumin**

1 For naan, combine flour, sugar, yeast and 1 teaspoon kosher salt in bowl of KitchenAid stand mixer. Attach bowl and dough hook to mixer. Turn to speed 4; add water, ½ cup yogurt and 1 tablespoon oil. Mix until dough forms a ball. Reduce to speed 2; knead 5 minutes or until dough is smooth and elastic. Cover bowl with damp cloth. Let stand at room temperature about 2 hours or until doubled in size.

2 Turn out dough onto lightly floured surface. Divide dough into quarters; roll into balls. Roll each dough ball into thin 8-inch circle. Heat large cast iron skillet over medium-high heat. Add 1 tablespoon oil. Carefully transfer one dough circle to hot skillet; cook about 2 minutes or until dough is puffed and bottom is dark brown in patches. Turn and cook 2 minutes or until browned. Brush hot naan with ghee and sprinkle with sea salt. Repeat with remaining oil, dough, ghee and sea salt, reducing heat to medium if skillet is smoking too much.

3 For sauce, combine 1 cup yogurt, cilantro, harissa, ½ teaspoon kosher salt and cumin in medium bowl. Serve with warm naan.

Tip: For a main dish, spread some of sauce over naan bread and top with grilled chicken strips. Sprinkle with chopped fresh cilantro, chopped cucumbers, tomatoes and/or onions.

Cranberry Brie Bubble Bread

MAKES 12 SERVINGS

3 cups all-purpose flour

1 package (¼ ounce; 2¼ teaspoons) active dry yeast

1 teaspoon salt

1 cup warm water (105° to 110°F)

¼ cup plus 2 tablespoons unsalted butter, melted, divided

¾ cup finely chopped pecans or walnuts

¼ cup packed brown sugar

¼ teaspoon coarse salt

1 package (7 ounces) Brie cheese, cut into ¼-inch pieces

1 cup whole-berry cranberry sauce

1 Combine flour, yeast and 1 teaspoon salt in bowl of KitchenAid stand mixer. Attach bowl and flat beater to mixer. Add warm water and 2 tablespoons melted butter; mix on speed 2 until rough dough forms. Replace flat beater with dough hook. Turn mixer to Stir speed; knead speed 5 to 7 minutes or until dough is smooth and elastic.

2 Shape dough into a ball. Place in large lightly greased bowl; turn to grease top. Cover and let rise in warm place about 45 minutes or until doubled in size.

3 Grease 2-quart baking dish or ovenproof bowl. Combine pecans, brown sugar and coarse salt in shallow bowl; mix well. Place remaining ¼ cup butter in another shallow bowl. Turn out dough onto lightly floured surface; pat and stretch into 9×6-inch rectangle. Cut dough into 1-inch pieces; roll into balls.

4 Dip balls of dough in butter; roll in pecan mixture to coat. Place in prepared baking dish, layering with Brie and spoonfuls of cranberry sauce. Cover and let rise in warm place about 45 minutes or until dough is puffy. Preheat oven to 350°F.

5 Bake 30 minutes or until dough is firm and filling is bubbly. Cool on wire rack 15 to 20 minutes. Serve warm.

Pull-Apart Potato Rolls

MAKES 18 ROLLS

1 **large russet baking potato, peeled and cut into 1-inch pieces**

2¼ **cups bread flour**

3 **tablespoons roasted garlic paste**

1 **tablespoon sugar**

1 **tablespoon chopped fresh rosemary**

1 **package (¼ ounce; 2¼ teaspoons) active dry yeast**

1 **teaspoon salt**

2 **eggs, divided**

1 **tablespoon unsalted butter, softened**

1 Place potatoes in small saucepan; cover with cold water. Bring to a boil over high heat. Reduce heat to low; simmer 8 to 10 minutes or until tender. Drain potatoes, reserving ¼ cup cooking liquid. Return potatoes to saucepan and cook over low heat 1 to 2 minutes or until dry.

2 Place potatoes in bowl of KitchenAid stand mixer. Attach bowl and flat beater to mixer. Turn to Speed 2; mix 30 seconds or until mashed. Measure 1 packed cup of mashed potatoes; discard remaining potatoes.

3 Place flour, garlic paste, sugar, rosemary, yeast, salt and 1 cup potatoes in mixer bowl. Replace flat beater with dough hook. Turn to Speed 2 and mix 1 to 2 minutes or until combined. Add 1 egg and reserved potato cooking liquid. Turn to speed 2; knead 8 to 10 minutes or until dough is soft and slightly sticky. Shape dough into a ball and place in large lightly greased bowl; turn to grease top. Cover and let rise in warm place 30 to 40 minutes or until almost doubled in size.

4 Line 13×9-inch baking pan with parchment paper. Grease bottom and sides with butter.

5 Turn out dough onto work surface, dusting with flour only if too sticky to handle. Pat gently into 12×8-inch rectangle. Cut into 18 equal pieces. Shape each piece into a ball and place in prepared pan, spacing evenly apart in 3 rows by 6 rows. Cover and let rise 30 to 40 minutes.

6 Preheat oven to 400°F. Beat remaining egg with 1 teaspoon water and brush over surface of rolls. Bake 14 to 18 minutes or until golden brown. Cool slightly before pulling apart.

Focaccia with Squash and Olives

MAKES 1 LOAF

1 **cup warm water (105° to 110°F)**

1 **tablespoon sugar**

1 **package (¼ ounce; 2¼ teaspoons) active dry or instant yeast**

3 **cups all-purpose flour**

1½ **teaspoons salt**

¼ **cup olive oil, plus additional for pan**

Cornmeal

1 **small zucchini, ends trimmed and cut into 3-inch pieces**

1 **yellow squash, ends trimmed and cut into 3-inch pieces**

⅔ **cup shredded Parmesan cheese**

½ **cup mixed olives**

1 **teaspoon dried oregano**

½ **teaspoon freshly ground black pepper**

1 Combine water, sugar and yeast in small bowl; stir to dissolve yeast. Let stand 5 minutes.

2 Combine flour and salt in bowl of KitchenAid stand mixer. Attach bowl and dough hook to mixer. Turn to Stir speed; mix 1 minute. Add yeast mixture and ¼ cup olive oil. Turn to speed 2; knead 4 minutes. Turn out dough onto floured surface; knead 5 to 6 times. Shape dough into a ball. Place in large lightly greased bowl; turn to grease top. Cover and let rise in warm place 1 hour or until doubled in size.

3 Grease 13×9-inch baking dish with olive oil; dust with cornmeal. Turn out dough onto floured surface. Pat and stretch dough into 13×9-inch rectangle; press into prepared pan. Cover and let rise 30 minutes.

4 Preheat oven to 425°F. Attach KitchenAid spiralizer to stand mixer. Place one zucchini piece on fruit and vegetable spike. Attach to mixer. Attach fine spiral blade and position at end of zucchini. Place medium bowl below blade to catch spiraled zucchini. Turn mixer to speed 3 and process until blade reaches end of zucchini. Repeat with remaining zucchini pieces and yellow squash.

5 Make indentations in dough with fingers. Sprinkle Parmesan cheese evenly over dough; top with zucchini, yellow squash and olives. Sprinkle with oregano and black pepper. Bake 20 to 25 minutes or until edges are golden brown. Cool slightly before serving.

Multigrain Loaf

MAKES 2 LOAVES

2½ cups warm water (105° to 110°F)

¼ cup honey

1½ tablespoons active dry yeast

3 cups whole wheat flour

3 cups bread flour

1 cup rye flour

½ cup cooked quinoa, at room temperature

¼ cup quick-cooking oats

¼ cup flax seeds

2 tablespoons whole-grain spelt

1 tablespoon salt

5 tablespoons salted butter, melted

1 Combine water, honey and yeast in small bowl; stir until yeast is dissolved. Let stand 10 minutes or until foamy.

2 Combine whole wheat flour, bread flour, rye flour, quinoa, oats, flax seeds, spelt and salt in bowl of KitchenAid stand mixer. Attach bowl and flat beater to mixer. Turn to speed 3; mix 1 minute. With mixer running on speed 3, drizzle in yeast mixture and butter; mix until just incorporated. Replace flat beater with dough hook. Turn to speed 2; knead 6 minutes. Place dough in large lightly greased bowl; turn to grease top. Cover and let rise in warm place 2 hours or until doubled in size.

3 Grease and flour two 9×5-inch loaf pans. Turn out dough onto lightly floured work surface; divide dough in half. Roll each dough piece into oblong 8-inch log. Place in prepared pans. Cover and let rise in warm place 45 minutes or until dough reaches tops of pans.

4 Preheat oven to 400°F. Bake 40 minutes. Remove from pans; cool completely on wire rack.

Tip: For an attractive presentation, brush top of loaves with egg wash and sprinkle with additional oats, rye, spelt or quinoa just before baking.

Monkey Bread

MAKES 10 TO 12 SERVINGS

¾ cup warm water (105° to 110°F)

1 package (¼ ounce; 2¼ teaspoons) active dry yeast

2 cups bread flour

½ cup all-purpose flour

2 tablespoons sugar

1 tablespoon ground toasted fennel seed

1 teaspoon salt

1¼ cups (2½ sticks) salted butter, melted, divided

2 cups grated Parmesan cheese

4 ounces fresh Italian sausage links, casings removed

¼ cup chopped fresh cilantro

¼ cup chopped fresh parsley

2 tablespoons chopped fresh thyme

1 Combine water and yeast in in small bowl; stir to dissolve yeast. Let stand 10 minutes or until foamy.

2 Combine bread flour, all-purpose flour, sugar, fennel and salt in bowl of KitchenAid stand mixer. Attach bowl and flat beater to mixer. Turn to Speed 3; mix 1 minute or until combined. With mixer running, add yeast mixture and ¼ cup melted butter; mix until just incorporated. Replace flat beater with dough hook. Turn to speed 2; knead 7 minutes. Place dough in large lightly greased bowl; turn to grease top. Cover and let rise in warm place 1 hour or until doubled in size.

3 Place cheese, remaining 1 cup melted butter, sausage, cilantro, parsley and thyme in mixer bowl. Attach bowl and flat beater to mixer. Turn to speed 3; mix 3 minutes or until smooth and glossy.

4 Grease and flour two 9×5-inch loaf pans. Turn out dough onto lightly floured surface. Shape dough into 1-inch balls. Dip each ball into sausage mixture; arrange in prepared pans, layering with additional sausage mixture. Cover and let rise in warm place 45 minutes.

5 Preheat oven to 350°F. Bake 40 minutes. Remove from pans; cool on wire rack 45 minutes. Serve warm. Store leftovers in the refrigerator.

Tip: Substitute ¼ cup dried Italian herbs for the combination of fresh cilantro, parsley and thyme.

Homemade Brioche

MAKES 1 LOAF

- **3 tablespoons warm whole milk (105° to 110°F)**
- **1½ teaspoons active dry yeast**
- **2½ cups all-purpose flour**
- **¼ cup sugar**
- **¾ teaspoon salt**
- **5 eggs**
- **1 cup (2 sticks) plus 2 tablespoons butter, cut into small pieces, softened**
- **1 teaspoon smoked salt flakes or regular flaky sea salt**

1 Combine milk and yeast in small bowl; stir until yeast is dissolved. Let stand 10 minutes or until foamy.

2 Combine flour, sugar and ¾ teaspoon salt in bowl of KitchenAid stand mixer. Attach bowl and dough hook to mixer. Turn to speed 2; mix until combined. With mixer running, add eggs and yeast mixture. Mix 8 minutes or until dough is uniform in texture. Scrape bottom and side of bowl. Turn mixer to speed 2; gradually add pieces of butter, mixing well after each addition. When all the butter is added, turn to speed 4. Mix 10 to 15 minutes or until dough is smooth and shiny. Remove bowl from mixer. Cover and let rise in warm place 2 hours or until doubled in size.

3 Grease 8×5-inch loaf pan. Turn out dough onto floured surface. Gently shape into oblong loaf. Place in prepared pan. Cover and let rise at room temperature 40 to 50 minutes.

4 Preheat oven to 400°F. Sprinkle top of loaf with smoked salt. Bake 45 to 50 minutes or until golden brown.

Tip: Dough can also be used to make individual buns. Prepare dough as directed and let rise once. Instead of shaping into a loaf, use an ice cream scoop to portion dough onto lightly greased parchment paper-lined baking sheet 2 inches apart. Grease hands and shape each dough ball into uniform round shape. Place on greased baking sheet. Cover and let rise at room temperature until doubled in size. Bake 15 to 20 minutes.

Parmesan-Herb Bagels

MAKES 10 SERVINGS

BAGELS

- 1½ **cups warm water (105° to 110°F)**
- 3 **tablespoons honey, divided**
- 1 **package (¼ ounce; 2¼ teaspoons) active dry yeast**
- 4 **cups bread flour**
- ½ **cup shredded Parmesan cheese**
- ½ **cup French fried onions**
- 2 **tablespoons chopped fresh chives**
- 2 **teaspoons chopped fresh thyme**
- 3 **tablespoons packed brown sugar, divided**
- 2 **teaspoons salt**
- 2 **quarts water**

TOPPING

- 1 **egg, beaten**
- 2 **teaspoons sea salt**
- ½ **cup French fried onions**
- 1 **cup shredded Parmesan cheese**

1 For bagels, combine 1½ cups warm water, 1 tablespoon honey and yeast in small bowl; stir until yeast is dissolved. Let stand 10 minutes or until foamy.

2 Combine flour, ½ cup cheese, ½ cup fried onions, chives, thyme, 1 tablespoon brown sugar and salt in bowl of KitchenAid stand mixer. Attach bowl and flat beater to mixer. Turn to Speed 2; mix 1 minute. With mixer running, add yeast mixture; mix until just incorporated. Replace flat beater with dough hook. Turn to Speed 2; knead 7 minutes. Place dough in large lightly greased bowl; turn to grease top. Cover and let rise in warm place about 1 hour or until doubled in size.

3 Turn out dough onto lightly floured surface. Cut into ten equal pieces. Roll each piece into a ball. Place on baking sheet. Cover and let rise 45 minutes.

4 Preheat oven to 400°F. Grease two baking sheets or line with parchment paper. Combine 2 quarts water, remaining 2 tablespoons brown sugar and remaining 2 tablespoons honey in large saucepan. Bring to a boil.

5 Poke a hole in center of each dough ball with finger; twirl and stretch dough until center hole is 2 to 2½ inches in diameter. Drop bagels, two at a time, into boiling water. Cook 1 minute on each side. Remove from water with strainer or tongs; place on prepared baking sheets.

6 For topping, brush tops of bagels with egg. Sprinkle evenly with sea salt, ½ cup fried onions and 1 cup cheese.

7 Bake 20 to 25 minutes or until puffed and golden brown, turning over after 15 minutes to ensure even browning. Cool on wire rack.

Cranberry and Walnut Bread

MAKES 8 TO 10 SERVINGS

¼ **cup warm water (105° to 110°F)**

1 **package (¼ ounce; 2¼ teaspoons) active dry yeast**

3½ **cups all-purpose flour**

1 **cup dried cranberries, coarsely chopped**

¾ **cup walnuts, chopped**

¼ **cup sugar**

½ **teaspoon salt**

½ **teaspoon black pepper**

¾ **cup cranberry juice**

¼ **cup (½ stick) salted butter, melted**

1 Combine water and yeast in small bowl; stir to dissolve yeast. Let stand 10 minutes until foamy.

2 Combine flour, cranberries, walnuts, sugar, salt and pepper in bowl of KitchenAid stand mixer. Attach bowl and flat beater to mixer. Turn to speed 3; mix 1 minute or until just combined. With mixer running, drizzle in yeast mixture, cranberry juice and melted butter; mix just until incorporated. Replace flat beater with dough hook. Turn to speed 2; knead 7 minutes. Place dough in large lightly greased bowl; turn to grease top. Cover and let rise in warm place 2 hours or until doubled in size.

3 Grease 8×4-inch loaf pan. Turn out dough onto lightly floured work surface. Roll dough into 12×8-inch rectangle. Fold dough in thirds to make 8×4-inch loaf; place in prepared pan. Cover and let rise in warm place 40 minutes or until doubled in size.

4 Preheat oven to 350°F. Bake 30 minutes or until lightly browned. Cool in pan on wire rack 20 minutes. Remove from pan; cool completely before slicing.

Quick Breads and Doughnuts

Loaded Banana Bread

MAKES 1 LOAF

- **6 tablespoons (¾ stick) butter, softened**
- **⅓ cup granulated sugar**
- **⅓ cup packed brown sugar**
- **2 eggs**
- **3 ripe bananas, mashed**
- **½ teaspoon vanilla**
- **1½ cups all-purpose flour**
- **2½ teaspoons baking powder**
- **¼ teaspoon salt**
- **1 can (8 ounces) crushed pineapple, drained**
- **⅓ cup flaked coconut**
- **¼ cup mini chocolate chips**
- **⅓ cup chopped walnuts (optional)**

1 Preheat oven to 350°F. Grease 9×5-inch loaf pan. Whisk flour, baking powder and salt in small bowl.

2 Combine butter, granulated sugar and brown sugar in bowl of KitchenAid stand mixer. Attach bowl and flat beater to mixer. Turn to speed 6; beat 4 minutes or until light and fluffy. Beat in eggs one at a time, beating well after each addition. Add bananas and vanilla. Turn to speed 2; gradually add flour mixture, beating just until blended.

3 Fold in pineapple, coconut and chocolate chips with spatula. Spoon batter into prepared pan. Top with walnuts, if desired.

4 Bake 50 minutes or until toothpick inserted into center comes out almost clean. Cool in pan on wire rack 1 hour. Remove to wire rack; cool completely.

Buttermilk Old-Fashioned Doughnuts

MAKES 14 DOUGHNUTS AND 14 DOUGHNUT HOLES

DOUGHNUTS

- 4½ **cups all-purpose flour**
- 4 **teaspoons baking powder**
- 2 **teaspoons salt**
- 1 **cup plus 2 tablespoons granulated sugar**
- 6 **egg yolks**
- 2½ **tablespoons butter**
- 1¼ **cups sour cream**
- ¼ **cup buttermilk**
  Vegetable oil for frying

GLAZE*

- 3½ **cups powdered sugar**
- ¼ **cup milk**
- ¼ **cup buttermilk**
- 1 **teaspoon salt**

To make chocolate glaze, replace ¼ cup of the powdered sugar with ¼ cup cocoa powder.

1 Spray medium bowl with nonstick cooking spray, line with plastic wrap and spray plastic wrap.

2 Whisk flour, baking powder and 2 teaspoons salt in large bowl.

3 Combine granulated sugar, egg yolks and butter in bowl of KitchenAid stand mixer. Attach bowl and flat beater to mixer. Turn to speed 2; mix 30 seconds. Turn to speed 10; beat 1 to 2 minutes or until light and fluffy. Add sour cream and ¼ cup buttermilk. Turn to speed 5; mix 1 to 2 minutes or until smooth. With mixer running on speed 3, add dry ingredients, ½ cup at a time, mixing well after each addition.

4 Place dough in prepared bowl. Spray top of dough with cooking spray; fold plastic wrap over dough. Refrigerate 1 hour.

5 Line baking sheet with parchment paper and spray with cooking spray. Turn out dough onto lightly floured work surface. Dust top of dough with flour and roll to ½-inch thickness. Cut out 14 circles using 3-inch round cutter. Cut out center holes using 1¼-inch round cutter, dipping cutters in flour before each use. (Or use doughnut cutter.)

6 Arrange doughnuts and holes on prepared baking sheet. Cover lightly with plastic wrap. Refrigerate 30 minutes.

7 Line wire racks with paper towels. Pour 2 inches of oil in large heavy saucepan; clip deep-fry or candy thermometer to side of pan. Heat over medium-high heat to 340°F. Working in batches, add doughnuts to hot oil. When doughnuts float to surface, cook 40 seconds then flip over gently using tongs or slotted spoon. Cook 1 minute; flip over and cook 1 minute or until doughnuts are golden brown. Do not crowd the pan and adjust heat to maintain temperature during frying. Remove with tongs to prepared wire rack. Repeat with doughnut holes. Cool 10 minutes.

8 For glaze, whisk powdered sugar, milk, ¼ cup buttermilk and 1 teaspoon salt in medium bowl until smooth. Dip doughnuts and doughnut holes into glaze; place on wire rack. Let stand until glaze is set.

Tip: Dough can be kept tightly wrapped in refrigerator for up to 1 week before rolling and frying. Cut doughnuts can be frozen up to 1 month. Thaw in refrigerator before frying.

Cinnamon Date Scones

MAKES 12 SCONES

2 cups all-purpose flour

2 tablespoons granulated sugar

2½ teaspoons baking powder

½ teaspoon salt

½ teaspoon ground cinnamon

5 tablespoons cold unsalted butter, cut into pieces

½ cup chopped pitted dates

2 eggs

⅓ cup heavy whipping cream or milk

Coarse sugar

1 Preheat oven to 425°F.

2 Combine flour, granulated sugar, baking powder, salt and cinnamon in bowl of KitchenAid stand mixer. Attach bowl and flat beater to mixer. Turn mixer to Stir speed; mix 1 minute. Add butter; mix on Stir speed until mixture resembles coarse crumbs. Stir in dates.

3 Whisk eggs in small bowl. Add cream; whisk until well blended. Reserve 1 tablespoon egg mixture in small bowl for brushing. Add remaining egg to flour mixture. Turn mixture to Stir speed; mix until dough clings together.

4 Turn out dough onto floured surface. Knead gently 10 times. Roll dough into 9×6-inch rectangle. Cut rectangle into six 3-inch squares. Cut each square diagonally in half. Place triangles 2 inches apart on ungreased baking sheet. Brush with reserved egg mixture; sprinkle with coarse sugar.

5 Bake 10 to 12 minutes or until golden brown. Immediately remove to wire rack. Cool slightly; serve warm.

Rhubarb Bread

MAKES 1 LOAF

2 cups all-purpose flour

1 cup sugar

1 tablespoon baking powder

1 teaspoon salt

¼ teaspoon ground cinnamon

1 cup milk

2 eggs

⅓ cup (5 tablespoons) unsalted butter, melted

2 teaspoons grated fresh ginger (about 1 inch)

2¼ cups chopped fresh rhubarb (¼-inch pieces)

¾ cup chopped walnuts, toasted*

*To toast walnuts, spread on ungreased baking sheet. Bake in preheated 350°F oven 6 to 8 minutes or until lightly browned, stirring frequently.

1 Preheat oven to 350°F. Grease 9×5-inch loaf pan.

2 Combine flour, sugar, baking powder, salt and cinnamon in bowl of KitchenAid stand mixer. Attach bowl and flat beater to mixer. Turn mixer to Stir speed; mix until well blended. Whisk milk, eggs, butter and ginger in medium bowl until well blended. Add to flour mixture. Turn to Stir speed; mix just until dry ingredients are moistened. Add rhubarb and walnuts; stir just until blended. Pour batter into prepared pan.

3 Bake 60 to 65 minutes or until toothpick inserted into center comes out clean. Cool in pan on wire rack 15 minutes. Remove to wire rack; cool completely.

Blueberry Coffee Cake Muffins

MAKES 12 MUFFINS

STREUSEL TOPPING

- ½ cup all-purpose flour
- ¼ cup packed brown sugar
- 2 tablespoons granulated sugar
- ¼ teaspoon salt
- ¼ cup (½ stick) cold unsalted butter, cut into small pieces

MUFFINS

- 1¼ cups granulated sugar
- ¾ cup plus 2 tablespoons vegetable oil
- 2½ cups all-purpose flour
- 2 tablespoons baking powder
- ½ teaspoon salt
- ¼ teaspoon baking soda
- ¾ cup sour cream
- 3 eggs
- 1 teaspoon grated lemon peel
- 1 teaspoon vanilla
- 1 pint fresh blueberries

1 Preheat oven to 350°F. Line 12 standard (2½-inch) muffin pan cups with paper baking cups; spray lightly with nonstick cooking spray.

2 For streusel topping, combine ½ cup flour, brown sugar, 2 tablespoons granulated sugar and ¼ teaspoon salt in bowl of KitchenAid stand mixer. Attach bowl and flat beater to mixer. Turn to Stir speed; mix 1 to 2 minutes or until well combined. Add butter; mix 1 minute or until mixture resembles coarse crumbs. Transfer to small bowl.

3 For muffins, place 1¼ cups sugar and oil in mixer bowl. Attach bowl and flat beater to mixer. Turn to speed 2; mix 2 minutes or until well blended.

4 Whisk 2½ cups flour, baking powder, ½ teaspoon salt and baking soda in medium bowl. Add to sugar mixture. Turn to Stir speed; mix 1 minute or just until combined. With mixer running, add sour cream, eggs, lemon peel and vanilla; mix 1 minute or until well blended.

5 Fill each muffin cup half full with batter. Top with 5 or 6 blueberries and 2 teaspoons streusel topping. Repeat layers of batter, berries and streusel to fill cups completely.

6 Bake 20 to 25 minutes or until tops are golden brown and toothpick inserted into centers comes out clean.

Tip: Substitute raspberries or mixed berries for the blueberries.

Glazed Lemon Loaf

MAKES 1 LOAF

BREAD

- 1½ **cups all-purpose flour**
- ½ **teaspoon baking powder**
- ½ **teaspoon baking soda**
- ½ **teaspoon salt**
- 1 **cup granulated sugar**
- 3 **eggs**
- ½ **cup vegetable oil**
- ⅓ **cup fresh lemon juice**
- 2 **tablespoons unsalted butter, melted**
- 1 **teaspoon lemon extract**
- ½ **teaspoon vanilla**

GLAZE

- 3 **tablespoons unsalted butter**
- 1½ **cups powdered sugar**
- 2 **tablespoons fresh lemon juice**
- 1 **to 2 teaspoons grated lemon peel**

1 Preheat oven to 350°F. Grease and flour 8×4-inch loaf pan.

2 For bread, combine flour, baking powder, baking soda and salt in large bowl; whisk until well blended. Place granulated sugar, eggs, oil, ⅓ cup lemon juice, 2 tablespoons melted butter, lemon extract and vanilla in bowl of KitchenAid stand mixer. Attach bowl and flat beater to mixer. Turn to speed 3; mix until well blended. Add flour mixture. Turn to Stir speed; mix just until blended. Pour batter into prepared pan.

3 Bake about 40 minutes or until toothpick inserted into center comes out clean. Cool in pan on wire rack 10 minutes. Remove to wire rack; cool 10 minutes.

4 For glaze, melt 3 tablespoons butter in small saucepan over medium-low heat. Whisk in powdered sugar, 2 tablespoons lemon juice and 1 teaspoon lemon peel; cook until smooth and hot, whisking constantly. Pour glaze over warm bread; smooth top. Garnish with additional 1 teaspoon lemon peel, if desired. Cool completely before slicing.

English-Style Scones

MAKES 6 SCONES

- **3 eggs, divided**
- **½ cup heavy whipping cream**
- **1½ teaspoons vanilla**
- **2 cups all-purpose flour**
- **2 teaspoons baking powder**
- **½ teaspoon salt**
- **¼ cup (½ stick) cold unsalted butter**
- **¼ cup finely chopped pitted dates**
- **¼ cup golden raisins or currants**
- **1 teaspoon water**
- **6 tablespoons orange marmalade**
- **Crème fraîche or whipped butter**

1. Preheat oven to 375°F. Line baking sheet with parchment paper.

2. Whisk 2 eggs, cream and vanilla in medium bowl until blended. Combine flour, baking powder and salt in bowl of KitchenAid stand mixer. Attach bowl and flat beater to mixer. Turn to speed 2; mix until mixture resembles coarse crumbs. Stir in dates and raisins. With mixer running on Stir speed, drizzle in cream mixture; mix just until moistened.

3. Turn out dough onto lightly floured surface; knead four times with floured hands. Place dough on prepared baking sheet; pat into 8-inch circle. Gently score dough into six wedges with sharp wet knife, cutting three-fourths of the way through dough. Beat remaining egg and water in small bowl; brush lightly over dough.

4. Bake 18 to 20 minutes or until golden brown. Cool on baking sheet on wire rack 5 minutes. Cut into wedges along score lines. Serve warm with marmalade and crème fraîche.

Toasted Coconut Doughnuts

MAKES 14 TO 16 DOUGHNUTS

2¾ **cups all-purpose flour**

¼ **cup cornstarch**

1½ **teaspoons baking powder**

1 **teaspoon salt**

½ **teaspoon ground cinnamon**

½ **teaspoon ground nutmeg**

1 **cup granulated sugar**

2 **eggs**

¼ **cup (½ stick) unsalted butter, melted**

¼ **cup applesauce**

1 **teaspoon vanilla**

¾ **cup coconut milk, divided***

Vegetable oil for frying

1 **cup flaked coconut**

1 **teaspoon dark rum or vanilla**

1½ **cups sifted powdered sugar**

*Shake the can vigorously to blend before opening the can. Or pour into medium bowl and whisk until homogenous.

1 Whisk 2¼ cups flour, cornstarch, baking powder, salt, cinnamon and nutmeg in large bowl.

2 Combine granulated sugar and eggs in bowl of KitchenAid stand mixer. Attach bowl and flat beater to mixer. Turn mixer to speed 10; beat 3 minutes or until pale and thick. Add butter, applesauce and vanilla. Turn to Stir speed; mix until blended. With mixer running, add flour mixture alternately with ½ cup coconut milk. Press plastic wrap directly onto surface of dough in mixer bowl; refrigerate at least 1 hour.

3 Pour about 2 inches of oil into Dutch oven or large heavy saucepan; clip deep-fry or candy thermometer to side of pot. Heat over medium-high heat to 360°F to 370°F.

4 Meanwhile, generously flour work surface. Turn out dough onto work surface and dust top with flour. Roll out dough to about ¼-inch thickness; cut out doughnuts with floured doughnut cutter. Gather and reroll scraps. Line large wire rack with paper towels.

5 Working in batches, add doughnuts to hot oil. Cook 1 minute per side or until golden brown. Do not crowd the pan and adjust heat to maintain temperature during frying. Remove with tongs or slotted spoon to prepared wire racks.

6 Spread coconut in large skillet; cook over medium-low heat about 10 minutes or until mostly golden brown, stirring frequently. Whisk remaining ¼ cup coconut milk and rum in medium bowl. Stir in powdered sugar to form smooth, thick glaze. Dip tops of doughnuts in glaze, letting excess drip back into bowl; immediately dip in coconut. Let stand until glaze is set.

Blueberry Scones

MAKES 8 SERVINGS

- ¾ **cup sour cream**
- ½ **cup plus 2 tablespoons buttermilk, divided**
- ¼ **cup granulated sugar**
- 1 **teaspoon vanilla**
- 1 **teaspoon grated lemon peel**
- ¾ **teaspoon fresh lemon juice, divided**
- ½ **teaspoon grated orange peel**
- 2½ **cups all-purpose flour**
- 4½ **teaspoons baking powder**
- 1 **teaspoon salt**
- ½ **cup (1 stick) plus 2 tablespoons cold unsalted butter, cut into small pieces**
- ½ **cup dried blueberries**
- 1 **egg**
- 1 **tablespoon water**
- 1 **teaspoon turbinado sugar**
- 1½ **cups powdered sugar**

1 Whisk sour cream, ½ cup buttermilk, granulated sugar, vanilla, lemon peel, ½ teaspoon lemon juice and orange peel in large bowl until well blended.

2 Combine flour, baking powder and salt in bowl of KitchenAid stand mixer. Attach bowl and flat beater to mixer. Turn to Stir speed; add butter and mix 1 minute or until mixture resembles coarse crumbs. Add sour cream mixture. Turn to Stir speed; mix 10 seconds or just until dough forms. Add blueberries. Turn to Stir speed; mix just until combined.

3 Turn out dough onto floured work surface. Gently shape into 1-inch-thick disc. Wrap dough in plastic wrap and refrigerate at least 2 hours or overnight.

4 Preheat oven to 350°F. Line baking sheet with parchment paper. Beat egg and 1 tablespoon water in small bowl. Cut dough into eight wedges. Place on prepared baking sheet. Brush with egg mixture and sprinkle with turbinado sugar. Bake 20 to 25 minutes or until tops are golden brown. Cool on wire rack.

5 Whisk powdered sugar, remaining 2 tablespoons buttermilk and ¼ teaspoon lemon juice in small bowl until smooth. Drizzle over scones.

Coffee Cakes

Classic Cinnamon Buns

MAKES 12 BUNS

DOUGH

- **1 cup warm milk (105° to 110°F)**
- **1 package (¼ ounce; 2¼ teaspoons) active dry yeast**
- **2 eggs**
- **½ cup granulated sugar**
- **¼ cup (½ stick) unsalted butter, softened**
- **1 teaspoon salt**
- **4 to 4¼ cups all-purpose flour**

FILLING

- **1 cup packed brown sugar**
- **3 tablespoons ground cinnamon**
- **Pinch of salt**
- **6 tablespoons (¾ stick) unsalted butter, softened**

ICING

- **1½ cups powdered sugar**
- **3 ounces cream cheese, softened**
- **¼ cup (½ stick) unsalted butter, softened**
- **½ teaspoon vanilla**
- **⅛ teaspoon salt**

1 Combine milk and yeast in bowl of KitchenAid stand mixer; stir until dissolved. Let stand 10 minutes or until foamy.

2 Add eggs, granulated sugar, ¼ cup butter and 1 teaspoon salt to yeast mixture. Attach bowl and flat beater to mixer. Turn to speed 5; beat until well blended. Add 4 cups flour. Turn to Stir speed; mix until dough begins to come together. Replace flat beater with dough hook. Turn to Stir speed; knead about 5 minutes or until smooth, elastic and slightly sticky. Add additional flour, 1 tablespoon at a time, if necessary to prevent sticking.

3 Shape dough into a ball. Place in large lightly greased bowl; turn to grease top. Cover and let rise in warm place about 1 hour or until doubled in size. Meanwhile for filling, combine brown sugar, cinnamon and pinch of salt in small bowl; mix well.

4 Grease 13×9-inch baking pan. Roll out dough into 18×14-inch rectangle on floured surface. Spread 6 tablespoons butter evenly over dough; top with cinnamon-sugar mixture. Beginning with long side, roll up dough tightly; pinch seam to seal. Cut log crosswise into 12 slices; place slices cut sides up in prepared pan. Cover and let rise in warm place about 30 minutes or until almost doubled in size. Preheat oven to 350°F.

5 Bake 20 to 25 minutes or until golden brown. Meanwhile for icing, combine powdered sugar, cream cheese, ¼ cup butter, vanilla and ⅛ teaspoon salt in mixer bowl. Attach bowl and flat beater to mixer. Turn to speed 4; beat 2 minutes or until smooth and creamy. Spread icing over warm cinnamon buns.

Cherry Coffee Cakes

MAKES 12 SERVINGS

DOUGH

- 2¼ **cups all-purpose flour**
- ½ **teaspoon salt**
- 1 **cup (2 sticks) cold unsalted butter, cut into pieces**
- 1 **cup sour cream**
- 1 **tablespoon fresh lemon juice**

FILLING

- 4 **ounces cream cheese, softened**
- ½ **cup powdered sugar**
- 1 **egg yolk**
- ½ **teaspoon vanilla**
- ¼ **teaspoon grated orange peel**
- ⅛ **teaspoon salt**
- 1 **can (14 ounces) cherry pie filling**
- 1 **whole egg**
- 1 **tablespoon water**

1 For dough, combine flour and ½ teaspoon salt in bowl of KitchenAid stand mixer. Add butter. Attach bowl and flat beater to mixer. Turn to speed 2; mix until mixture resembles coarse crumbs. Add sour cream and lemon juice. Turn to Stir speed; mix just until dough forms.

2 Turn dough onto floured surface; press into a ball. Wrap with plastic wrap; refrigerate at least 3 hours or overnight.

3 For filling, place cream cheese in mixer bowl. Attach bowl and flat beater to mixer. Turn to speed 2; mix 1 minute or until smooth. Add powdered sugar, egg yolk, vanilla, orange peel and salt. Turn to Stir speed; mix 1 minute or until smooth and well blended.

4 Preheat oven to 400°F. Line baking sheet with parchment paper. Roll out dough on lightly floured surface to ¼-inch thickness. Cut out 24 circles using 3¼-inch round cutter. Place half of dough circles on prepared baking sheet; prick all over with fork. Cut out centers from remaining circles with 2¼-inch round cutter, creating a ring shape. Place dough rings on top of dough circles on baking sheet. (Discard small inner circles).

5 Spoon filling evenly into centers of pastries. Top with about 6 cherries and dab of sauce. Beat whole egg and 1 tablespoon water in small bowl. Brush top edge of pastries with egg mixture.

6 Bake 25 to 30 minutes or until golden brown. Remove to wire rack; cool completely.

Cardamom Rolls

MAKES 12 ROLLS

DOUGH

- ½ **cup water**
- ½ **cup milk**
- 1 **tablespoon active dry yeast**
- ½ **cup plus 1 teaspoon granulated sugar, divided**
- ½ **cup (1 stick) unsalted butter, softened**
- 3 **eggs**
- ½ **teaspoon vanilla**
- 4 **cups all-purpose flour, divided**
- ¾ **teaspoon salt**

FILLING

- 2 **tablespoons unsalted butter, very soft**
- ¼ **cup packed brown sugar**
- 1½ **teaspoons ground cardamom**
- 1 **teaspoon ground cinnamon**
- 1 **tablespoon unsalted butter, melted**
- **Pearl sugar (optional)**

1 Heat water and milk in small saucepan to about 110°F. Transfer to small bowl; stir in yeast and 1 teaspoon granulated sugar until dissolved. Let stand 5 minutes or until mixture is foamy.

2 Place ½ cup butter and remaining ½ cup granulated sugar in bowl of KitchenAid stand mixer. Attach bowl and flat beater to mixer. Turn to speed 6; beat 5 minutes or until light and fluffy. With mixer running on speed 5, add eggs one at a time, beating until well blended after each addition. Beat in vanilla. Scrape bottom and side of bowl. Turn mixer to Stir speed; add yeast mixture, 2 cups flour and salt. Increase to speed 5; beat 2 minutes.

3 Replace flat beater with dough hook. Add remaining 2 cups flour. Turn mixer to Stir speed; knead until most of flour is incorporated. Increase to speed 5; beat 3 minutes (dough will be sticky). Cover and let rise in warm place about 1½ hours or until doubled in size. Stir down dough. Cover and refrigerate 2 hours or overnight.

4 Turn out dough onto lightly floured surface. Roll out dough into 18-inch square. Spread 2 tablespoons butter over top half of dough. Sprinkle with brown sugar, cardamom and cinnamon. Fold bottom of dough over filling; pinch ends to seal. Roll into 20×10-inch rectangle. Cut dough crosswise into 12 strips. Cut each strip lengthwise into two or three pieces, leaving them connected at the top. Holding uncut end, wrap cut dough around fingers and pull into knot shape, turning to expose some of filling. Place on baking sheet. Brush with melted butter; sprinkle with pearl sugar, if desired. Let stand 15 minutes.

5 Preheat oven to 375°F. Bake 15 to 20 minutes or until golden brown. Cool on wire rack.

Apple Walnut Brunch Cake

MAKES 12 SERVINGS

3 **cups all-purpose flour**

1 **teaspoon baking soda**

1 **teaspoon salt**

1 **teaspoon ground cinnamon**

1 **cup chopped walnuts**

1½ **cups granulated sugar**

1 **cup vegetable oil**

2 **eggs**

2 **teaspoons vanilla**

2 **medium tart apples, peeled, cored and chopped**

Powdered sugar (optional)

1 Preheat oven to 325°F. Grease 10-inch tube pan or 12-cup bundt pan.

2 Whisk flour, baking soda, salt and cinnamon in large bowl. Stir in walnuts.

3 Place granulated sugar, oil, eggs and vanilla in bowl of KitchenAid stand mixer. Attach bowl and flat beater to mixer. Turn to Stir speed; mix until well blended. Stir in apples. Add flour mixture; mix on Stir speed until moistened. Spoon batter into prepared pan; smooth top.

4 Bake 1 hour or until toothpick inserted near center comes out clean. Cool cake in pan on wire rack 10 minutes. Loosen edges with metal spatula, if necessary. Turn out onto wire rack; cool completely.

5 Sprinkle with powdered sugar just before serving, if desired.

Sour Cream Coffee Cake

MAKES 16 SERVINGS

STREUSEL TOPPING AND FILLING

- ½ **cup all-purpose flour**
- ½ **cup granulated sugar**
- ½ **cup packed dark brown sugar, divided**
- 2 **tablespoons ground cinnamon**
- ¼ **teaspoon salt**
- 4 **tablespoons unsalted butter, cut into pieces**
- 1 **cup pecans, finely chopped**

CAKE

- 2½ **cups all-purpose flour**
- 2 **teaspoons baking powder**
- 1 **teaspoon baking soda**
- ½ **teaspoon salt**
- ¾ **cup (1½ sticks) unsalted butter, softened**
- 1 **cup granulated sugar**
- 4 **eggs**
- 1½ **cups sour cream**
- 1 **tablespoon vanilla**
- ½ **cup strawberry jam**

1 For filling, whisk ½ cup flour, ½ cup granulated sugar, ¼ cup brown sugar, cinnamon and ¼ teaspoon salt in medium bowl. Transfer half of mixture to bowl of KitchenAid stand mixer; stir remaining ¼ cup brown sugar into remaining mixture in medium bowl; set aside.

2 For topping, add butter to mixer bowl. Attach bowl and flat beater to mixer. Turn to Stir speed; mix until mixture resembles coarse crumbs. Stir in pecans. Transfer to small bowl; refrigerate until ready to use.

3 For cake, preheat oven to 350°F. Grease 9-inch square baking pan; line bottom with parchment paper. Whisk 2½ cups flour, baking powder, baking soda and ½ teaspoon salt in large bowl.

4 Place ¾ cup butter and 1 cup granulated sugar in mixer bowl. Attach bowl and flat beater to mixer. Turn to Stir speed; mix 30 seconds or until combined. Turn to speed 6; beat 3 minutes or until light and fluffy. Scrape bottom and side of bowl. Turn to speed 4; add eggs one at a time, mixing well after each addition. Add sour cream and vanilla; mix on speed 2 until smooth and well blended. Scrape bottom and side of bowl.

5 Turn mixer to Stir speed; add flour mixture in two additions, mixing just until blended. Place ½ cup batter in small bowl; whisk in jam. Spread half of remaining plain batter in prepared pan. Top with half of jam mixture. Sprinkle with filling. Spread remaining batter over filling; top with remaining jam mixture and sprinkle with topping.

6 Bake 45 to 50 minutes or until toothpick inserted into center comes out clean. Cool completely in pan on wire rack. Cut into squares.

Cherry, Almond and Chocolate Twist

MAKES 1 RING

BREAD

- **1** cup cold water
- **1** cup dried sweet or sour cherries
- **½** cup granulated sugar, divided
- **1** package (¼ ounce; 2¼ teaspoons) active dry yeast
- **¼** cup warm water (105° to 110°F)
- **½** cup warm milk (105° to 110°F)
- **3** tablespoons unsalted butter, cut into pieces
- **2** eggs, divided
- **1** tablespoon grated lemon peel
- **½** teaspoon salt
- **½** teaspoon almond extract
- **2½** to 2¾ cups all-purpose flour
- **½** cup canned almond filling (about 12 ounces)
- **¾** cup semisweet chocolate chips
- **1** tablespoon cold milk

ALMOND GLAZE

- **½** cup powdered sugar
- **2** teaspoons milk
- **¼** teaspoon almond extract

1 Combine cold water, cherries and ¼ cup granulated sugar in small saucepan; bring to a boil over high heat, stirring constantly. Remove from heat; cover and set aside.

2 Dissolve yeast in ¼ cup warm water in bowl of KitchenAid stand mixer; let stand 5 minutes or until bubbly.

3 Add milk, butter, remaining ¼ cup granulated sugar, 1 egg, lemon peel, salt and almond extract to yeast mixture. Attach bowl and flat beater to mixer. Turn to Stir speed; mix until well blended. Replace flat beater with dough hook. Add 2¼ cups flour. Turn mixer to speed 2; mix until dough forms a sticky ball. Add enough remaining flour to form soft dough; knead about 5 minutes or until dough is smooth and elastic, adding additional flour to prevent sticking if necessary. Shape dough into a ball. Place in large lightly greased bowl; turn to grease top. Cover and let rise in warm place about 1 hour or until doubled in size.

4 Preheat oven to 350°F. Line large baking sheet with parchment paper. Turn out dough onto lightly floured surface; knead 10 to 12 times or until dough is smooth. Shape dough into 10-inch log. Flatten slightly.

5 Roll out dough into 18×8-inch rectangle with lightly floured rolling pin. Drain cherries. Spread almond filling evenly over dough; sprinkle with cherries and chocolate chips. Starting with long side, tightly roll up dough. Pinch seam to seal.

6 Transfer rolled dough to prepared baking sheet. Use long sharp knife to cut roll in half lengthwise (through all layers). Turn halves cut sides up on baking sheet; carefully twist halves together, keeping cut sides facing up as much as possible. Press ends together to seal and tuck underneath. Whisk remaining egg and cold milk in small bowl until well blended. Brush lightly over dough.

7 Bake 30 minutes or until golden brown. (Cover loosely with foil if browning too quickly.) Cool on baking sheet 5 minutes. Remove to wire rack; cool completely.

8 For glaze, whisk ½ cup powdered sugar, 2 teaspoons milk and ¼ teaspoon almond extract in small bowl until smooth. Add additional milk, 1 teaspoon at a time, until glaze is of desired consistency; drizzle over coffeecake. Let stand until set.

Honey-Pecan Coffee Cake

MAKES 12 SERVINGS

⅔ **cup milk**

6 **tablespoons unsalted butter, softened**

9 **tablespoons honey, divided**

2½ **to 3½ cups all-purpose flour, divided**

1 **package (¼ ounce; 2¼ teaspoons) active dry yeast**

¾ **teaspoon salt**

3 **eggs, divided**

1¼ **cups coarsely chopped toasted* pecans, divided**

3 **tablespoons packed brown sugar**

1½ **tablespoons unsalted butter, melted**

1 **tablespoon ground cinnamon**

1 **teaspoon water**

*To toast nuts, spread in even layer on baking sheet. Bake at 350°F for 10 to 15 minutes or until golden brown, stirring once or twice.

1 Heat milk, softened butter and 3 tablespoons honey in small saucepan over low heat until temperature reaches 120° to 130°F. Combine 2¼ cups flour, yeast and salt in bowl of KitchenAid stand mixer. Attach bowl and flat beater to mixer. Turn mixer to Stir speed; gradually add warm milk mixture to flour mixture. Add 2 eggs; mix 2 minutes or until mixture is well blended. Scrape bottom and side of bowl. With mixer running on Stir speed, gradually add additional flour until soft dough forms.

2 Replace flat beater with dough hook. Turn to speed 2; knead 5 to 8 minutes or until smooth and elastic, adding remaining flour by tablespoons to prevent sticking, if necessary. Shape dough into a ball. Place in large lightly greased bowl; turn to grease top. Cover and let rise in warm place 35 to 40 minutes or until dough has increased in size by one third.

3 Turn out dough onto lightly floured surface. Roll into 14×8-inch rectangle with lightly floured rolling pin. Combine 1 cup pecans, brown sugar, melted butter, cinnamon and 3 tablespoons honey in small bowl. Spread evenly over dough; press in gently with fingertips. Starting from one long end, roll up tightly. Pinch seams to seal; turn seam side down. Flatten slightly. Twist dough 6 to 8 turns. Grease 9-inch cake pan. Place dough in pan in a loose spiral starting in center and working to the side. Tuck outside end under dough; pinch to seal. Loosely cover with lightly greased sheet of plastic wrap. Let rise in warm place about 1 hour or until doubled in size.

4 Preheat oven to 350°F. Place pan on baking sheet. Beat remaining egg and 1 teaspoon water in small bowl; brush all over dough. Drizzle remaining 3 tablespoons honey evenly over top; sprinkle with remaining ¼ cup pecans. Bake about 45 minutes or until deep golden brown. Turn pan and tent with sheet of foil halfway through baking time to prevent burning. Remove foil for last 5 minutes of baking. Cool in pan on wire rack 5 minutes. Remove from pan; cool completely on wire rack.

Entrées

Merguez Sausage

MAKES 8 SERVINGS

- **1 pound lamb shoulder or leg, cut into 1-inch cubes**
- **1 pound beef shoulder, cut into 1-inch pieces**
- **⅓ cup chopped fresh parsley**
- **2 tablespoons dried oregano**
- **2 teaspoons kosher salt**
- **1½ teaspoons smoked paprika**
- **1 teaspoon sugar**
- **1 teaspoon ground cumin**
- **1 teaspoon freshly ground black pepper**
- **½ teaspoon red pepper flakes**
- **1 cup roasted red peppers, finely diced**
- **3 tablespoons water**
- **2 tablespoons red wine**
- **3 cloves garlic, peeled**
- **5 feet large natural sausage casing***
- **1 tablespoon olive oil**
- **Lemon wedges and chopped fresh oregano**

Soak natural casings in cold water at least 30 minutes before using; rinse thoroughly.

1. Line baking sheet with parchment paper. Place lamb and beef on prepared baking sheet; freeze 20 minutes. Combine parsley, oregano, salt, paprika, sugar, cumin, black pepper and red pepper flakes in large bowl. Add meat; toss to coat. Add garlic.

2. Assemble KitchenAid food grinder with fine grinding plate; attach to KitchenAid stand mixer. Place mixer bowl under grinder. Turn mixer to speed 4; grind seasoned meat into bowl, taking care not to force it through. Stir roasted peppers, 3 tablespoons water and wine into meat mixture; use hands or spatula to mix well. Keep meat mixture cold.

3. Attach KitchenAid sausage stuffer with large stuffing tube to mixer. Grease sausage tube with olive oil or water; slide casings on tightly. Place 13×9-inch baking pan under sausage stuffer; add a few tablespoons of water to pan. Tie the end of casings into knot; pierce it with pin. Turn mixer to speed 4; slowly feed sausage mixture into hopper using food pusher. Hold tied end of casing in one hand and guide the sausage mixture as it fills casing. Do not pack too tightly in casing. Coil filled casing in pan; pinch 4-inch lengths, then twist six times into sausage links. Refrigerate in pan overnight.

4. To cook, heat olive oil in large skillet or cast iron skillet over medium-high heat. Separate sausage links; place in skillet and brown on all sides. Reduce heat to low; cook 15 to 20 minutes or until cooked through (160°F).

5. To grill, heat grill to medium heat. Add sausage links; cook 5 minutes. Turn and cook an additional 5 minutes or until cooked through (160°F). Squeeze lemon wedges over sausage and sprinkle with fresh oregano.

Fettuccine with Heirloom Tomatoes, Burrata and Balsamic

MAKES 4 TO 6 SERVINGS

PASTA

- **2 cups 00 pasta flour or all-purpose flour**
- **¼ teaspoon salt**
- **2 eggs**
- **1 teaspoon olive oil**
- **1 to 2 tablespoons water**
- **Semolina flour**

SAUCE

- **2 tablespoons olive oil**
- **4 cloves garlic, coarsely chopped**
- **3 cups chopped seeded heirloom tomatoes**
- **½ teaspoon sea salt**
- **¼ teaspoon freshly ground black pepper**
- **¼ cup torn fresh basil**
- **2 tablespoons chopped fresh parsley**
- **10 ounces burrata cheese**
- **2 tablespoons shredded Parmesan cheese**
- **Prepared balsamic glaze**

1 Place pasta flour and ¼ teaspoon salt in bowl of KitchenAid stand mixer. Attach bowl and flat beater to mixer. Turn to speed 2; mix 30 seconds. Make a well in the center of flour mixture; add eggs and olive oil. Turn to speed 2; mix 2 minutes. Add water 1 tablespoon at a time until dough holds together. Replace flat beater with dough hook. Turn to Stir speed; knead 2 to 3 minutes. Shape dough into a ball; wrap in plastic wrap and let rest at least 1 hour.

2 Attach KitchenAid pasta roller to mixer with adjustment knob set to 1. Divide dough into quarters and flatten one piece, keeping remaining dough wrapped to prevent drying out. Turn mixer to speed 2 and feed flattened dough through rollers to knead. Fold dough in half and roll again, repeating until dough is smooth and pliable and covers the width of the rollers. Change roller setting to 2 and feed dough sheet through rollers to flatten; do not fold dough for this step. Repeat for roller settings 3 to 6. Lightly dust pasta sheet with semolina flour and set aside. Repeat with remaining dough.

3 Replace roller attachment with fettuccine cutter. Turn to speed 2 and cut pasta sheets into noodles. Twirl into nests on parchment paper and dust with semolina flour. Let stand until ready to use.

4 For sauce, heat olive oil in large cast iron skillet over medium-high heat. Add garlic; sauté 1 minute or until lightly browned. Add tomatoes; cook 2 to 3 minutes until heated through. Stir in ½ teaspoon salt and pepper.

5 Bring large saucepan of salted water to a boil over high heat. Add pasta; cook 2 minutes or until al dente. Using tongs, remove pasta from water and transfer to skillet with sauce; cook 1 minute.

6 Transfer pasta to serving bowl. Sprinkle with basil and parsley; dollop with burrata. Sprinkle with Parmesan and lightly drizzle with balsamic glaze.

Tomato Basil Tart

MAKES 8 SERVINGS

TART DOUGH

- 1½ cups all-purpose flour
- ½ teaspoon salt, divided
- ½ teaspoon freshly ground pepper, divided
- ¼ teaspoon dried oregano
- 6 tablespoons cold unsalted butter, cut into pieces
- 1 egg
- 2 to 3 tablespoons ice water

FILLING

- 1 cup packed fresh basil leaves, plus 3 basil leaves, coarsely chopped, divided
- ½ cup pine nuts, toasted*
- 2 cloves garlic
- ¼ cup plus 1 tablespoon olive oil, divided
- 9 (¼-inch) slices fresh mozzarella
- 3 plum tomatoes, thinly sliced

Place pine nuts in small skillet. Heat over low heat 2 minutes or until light brown and fragrant, shaking occasionally.

1 Preheat oven to 400°F.

2 For dough, place flour, ¼ teaspoon salt, ¼ teaspoon pepper and oregano in bowl of KitchenAid stand mixer. Attach bowl and flat beater to mixer. Turn to Stir speed; mix until combined. Add butter; mix on speed 2 until mixture resembles coarse crumbs. Add egg and 2 tablespoons ice water; mix on speed 2 just until dough forms a ball. Add additional water if dough seems dry. Press dough into 12-inch rectangular tart pan with removable bottom. Prick bottom of crust all over with fork. Line with foil; fill with dried beans. Bake 20 minutes. Remove foil and beans; bake 4 minutes or until crust is light golden brown. Cool slightly.

3 For filling, combine 1 cup basil leaves, pine nuts, garlic, remaining ¼ teaspoon salt and ¼ teaspoon pepper in food processor. Drizzle with 1 tablespoon olive oil. Process about 10 seconds or until coarsely chopped. With motor running, drizzle in remaining ¼ cup olive oil. Process about 30 seconds or until almost smooth.**

4 Preheat broiler. Spread pesto evenly over crust. Layer with mozzarella and tomato slices. Sprinkle with additional salt and pepper. Broil 5 minutes or until cheese is melted. Sprinkle with chopped basil. Serve warm or at room temperature.

**Pesto can be made 1 week in advance. Transfer to covered container and store in refrigerator. Makes ½ cup pesto.

Pear Salad with Blue Cheese Dressing

MAKES 4 SERVINGS

DRESSING

- ½ **cup sour cream**
- ¼ **cup buttermilk**
- 1½ **teaspoons white wine vinegar**
- 1 **clove roasted garlic, mashed**
- ¼ **cup crumbled blue cheese, plus additional for serving**
- ¼ **teaspoon freshly ground black pepper**

SALAD

- 2 **Anjou pears**
- 4 **cups mixed greens, such as watercress, frisee and curly endive**
- ⅓ **cup roasted salted pumpkin seeds**

1 For dressing, whisk sour cream, buttermilk, vinegar and garlic in small bowl. Gently fold in ¼ cup blue cheese. Season with pepper. Refrigerate until ready to use (dressing can be made 1 day in advance).

2 Attach spiralizer to KitchenAid stand mixer. Center one pear on fruit and vegetable spike; attach to spiralizer. Attach spiral slice small core blade and position at end of pear. Turn mixer to speed 3; process until blade reaches end of pear. Stand pear on end on cutting board; cut in half to make half circles. Repeat with remaining pear.

3 Divide greens among four salad plates; top each with half a pear, pumpkin seeds and additional blue cheese. Serve with dressing.

Barbecue Chicken Pizza

MAKES 2 PIZZAS; 8 TO 10 SERVINGS

PIZZA DOUGH

- 3¼ cups bread flour
- 1 cup whole wheat flour
- 1 package (¼ ounce; 2¼ teaspoons) active dry yeast
- 1¼ teaspoons salt
- 1¾ cups warm water (105° to 110°F)
- 2 tablespoons olive oil
- Cornmeal

TOPPINGS

- 1 cup barbecue sauce
- 2 cups (8 ounces) shredded sharp Cheddar cheese
- ¼ red onion, thinly sliced
- 1 red bell pepper, thinly sliced
- 2 jalapeño peppers, seeded and sliced
- ¾ cup canned black beans, rinsed and drained
- 1 cup shredded rotisserie chicken
- 2 green onions, coarsely chopped
- ½ cup crisp-cooked crumbled bacon

1 For dough, combine bread flour, whole wheat flour, yeast and salt in bowl of KitchenAid stand mixer. Attach bowl and flat beater to mixer. Turn to speed 2; mix until well blended. With mixer running, pour in water and olive oil; mix until rough dough forms. Replace flat beater with dough hook. Turn to speed 2; knead 5 to 7 minutes or until dough is smooth and elastic, adding additional bread flour by teaspoons if needed. Shape dough into a ball. Place in large lightly greased bowl; turn to grease top. Cover and let rise in warm place about 1 hour or until doubled in size.

2 Punch down dough; let rest 15 minutes. Divide dough in half; shape into balls.

3 Preheat oven to 500°F. Preheat pizza stone in oven or line two baking sheets with parchment paper; dust parchment with cornmeal. Roll out dough to ¼-inch-thick circle on lightly floured surface. Transfer dough rounds to cornmeal-dusted pizza peels or place on prepared baking sheet.

4 Spread ½ cup barbecue sauce over each crust. Sprinkle each with ½ cup cheese and top with vegetables, black beans, chicken, green onions and bacon. Sprinkle with remaining cheese. Bake 8 to 10 minutes or until crust is golden and cheese is melted (bake one at a time on pizza stone). Cut into wedges to serve.

Steamed Pork Buns

MAKES 12 BUNS

PORK FILLING

- **1 pound ground pork**
- **⅓ cup onion and ginger sauce**
- **1 tablespoon light soy sauce**
- **1 tablespoon dark soy sauce**
- **1½ teaspoons cornstarch**
- **1 teaspoon sea salt**
- **1 teaspoon sugar**
- **1 teaspoon dark sesame oil**
- **⅛ teaspoon white pepper**

BUN WRAPPER

- **1 cup warm water (105° to 110°F)**
- **1 tablespoon sugar**
- **½ teaspoon instant or active dry yeast**
- **3 cups cake flour, divided**
- **½ teaspoon baking powder**
- **1½ teaspoons shortening or lard**

1 For filling, place pork, onion and ginger sauce, light soy sauce, dark soy sauce, cornstarch, salt, 1 teaspoon sugar, sesame oil and white pepper in bowl of KitchenAid stand mixer. Attach bowl and flat beater to mixer. Turn to Stir speed; mix 1 minute. Transfer to medium bowl. Cover with plastic wrap; refrigerate until ready to use.

2 For wrapper dough, combine water, 1 tablespoon sugar and yeast in small bowl, stirring to dissolve yeast; let stand 5 minutes.

3 Place 1½ cups flour, baking powder and shortening in clean mixer bowl. Attach bowl and flat beater to mixer. Turn mixer to speed 2; gradually add yeast mixture and mix 2 minutes. Replace flat beater with dough hook. Turn mixer to speed 2; add remaining flour ½ cup at a time until dough clings to hook and forms a ball. Knead 2 minutes.

4 Line baking sheet with parchment paper; dust with flour. Shape dough into a ball on lightly floured surface; let rest 10 minutes. Divide dough into 12 equal pieces. Roll each piece into a circle about 4 inches in diameter. Place 2 rounded tablespoons pork filling in center of circle. Gently pleat and shape wrapper around filling, pinching to seal at the top. Place on prepared baking sheet; let rest 20 to 30 minutes.

5 Fit steamer basket into large saucepan; fill saucepan with water to just below steamer basket. Bring to a gentle boil. Steam buns in batches 10 to 12 minutes or until cooked through. Serve immediately.

Deep-Dish Ham Quiche

MAKES 6 TO 8 SERVINGS

CRUST

1½ **cups all-purpose flour**

½ **cup (1 stick) cold salted butter, cut into small pieces**

½ **teaspoon salt**

¼ **cup water**

FILLING

1¼ **cups heavy whipping cream**

2 **whole eggs**

2 **egg yolks**

¼ **teaspoon salt**

⅛ **teaspoon ground white pepper**

1 **cup shredded Parmesan cheese**

1 **cup diced cooked ham**

6 **tablespoons chopped fresh chives**

1 For crust, combine flour, butter and ½ teaspoon salt in bowl of KitchenAid stand mixer. Attach bowl and flat beater to mixer. Turn to Stir speed; mix 3 minutes or until mixture resembles coarse crumbs. With mixer running, add water and mix 1 minute or until just combined. Wrap in plastic wrap and refrigerate 20 minutes.

2 Preheat oven to 350°F. Remove dough from refrigerator. Roll out to about 11-inch circle on lightly floured surface. Place dough in deep 9-inch pie pan. Trim and flute edge as needed. Pierce dough all over with fork. Cover with parchment paper and fill with dried beans or pie weights. Bake 10 minutes. Cool on wire rack. Remove beans and parchment paper.

3 For filling, place cream, whole eggs, egg yolks, ¼ teaspoon salt and pepper in mixer bowl. Attach bowl and wire whip to mixer. Turn to speed 3; mix until well blended. Spread Parmesan, ham and chives in crust. Pour in egg mixture.

4 Bake 30 to 35 minutes or until top is puffy and knife inserted into center comes out clean. Let stand 10 minutes before cutting.

Dijon and Dill Salmon Burgers

MAKES 8 TO 10 SERVINGS

3 cups diced raw salmon fillets (about 1½ pounds)

3 cups diced hot-smoked salmon (about ¾ pound)*

½ cup chopped fresh chives

¼ cup Dijon mustard

2 eggs

2 tablespoons chopped fresh dill

Salt

1 to 2 tablespoons olive oil

If hot-smoked salmon is not available, substitute additional diced raw salmon.

1 Combine salmon, chives, mustard, eggs and dill in bowl of KitchenAid stand mixer. Season with salt. Attach bowl and flat beater to mixer. Turn to Stir speed; mix 2 minutes or until just combined. Shape mixture into 8 to 10 (3½-ounce) patties.

2 Heat 1 tablespoon olive oil in large skillet over high heat. Cook patties, in batches, 3 to 5 minutes on each side for medium rare, adding additional olive oil if needed.

Tip: Check the saltiness of the smoked salmon before adding additional salt to the mixture.

Eggs Benedict

MAKES 4 SERVINGS

HOLLANDAISE SAUCE
- ½ **cup (1 stick) unsalted butter, cut into pieces**
- 4 **egg yolks**
- 1 **teaspoon water**
- 2 **teaspoons fresh lemon juice**
- 1 **dash hot pepper sauce**
  Salt and black pepper

EGGS
- 1 **teaspoon white vinegar**
- 8 **whole eggs**
- 8 **slices Canadian bacon**
- 4 **English muffins, split, toasted**

1 For hollandaise sauce, fill bowl of KitchenAid stand mixer halfway with boiling water. Let stand 2 minutes.

2 Melt butter in small saucepan over high heat.

3 Discard hot water and dry mixer bowl. Place egg yolks and 1 teaspoon water in bowl. Attach bowl and wire whip to mixer. Turn to speed 8; gradually add hot butter in thin steady stream. Whip 2 minutes. Mix in lemon juice and hot pepper sauce; season with salt. Pour into same saucepan; heat over low heat to 146°F. Keep warm.

4 For eggs, fill large saucepan with 3 inches of water. Bring to a gentle simmer over medium heat; add vinegar. Carefully crack eggs into water; cook 3 minutes. Remove with slotted spoon. Meanwhile, cook Canadian bacon in large skillet until browned on both sides.

5 Arrange 2 English muffin halves on each serving plate. Top with Canadian bacon, poached eggs and hollandaise sauce. Season with salt and black pepper, if desired. Serve immediately.

Pulled Pork

MAKES ABOUT 8 (1-CUP) SERVINGS

½ **cup packed brown sugar**

2 **teaspoons paprika**

2 **teaspoons salt**

2 **teaspoons ground cumin**

1 **teaspoon freshly ground black pepper**

¾ **teaspoon ground red pepper**

3 **cloves garlic, minced**

4 **to 5 pounds whole bone-in or boneless pork butt**

1 **tablespoon vegetable oil**

¾ **cup chopped sweet onion**

¾ **cup chicken broth, vegetable broth or water**

Hamburger buns, coleslaw and barbecue sauce (optional)

1 Preheat oven to 300°F. Combine brown sugar, paprika, salt, cumin, black pepper, ground red pepper and garlic in small bowl. Rub all over pork. Let sit 30 minutes.

2 Heat oil in large Dutch oven with tight fitting lid over medium-high heat. Add pork; brown on all sides, about 5 minutes total. Add onion; cook about 2 minutes or until onion is softened, stirring to scrape up browned bits from bottom of Dutch oven. Pour in broth; cover and transfer to oven.

3 Cook 2½ to 3 hours or until pork is beginning to become tender. Remove lid; continue to roast 1 to 2 hours or until crispy on the outside and very tender when tested with a fork. Remove from oven; let cool 20 minutes. Reserve pan juices.

4 Cut pork into 3 to 4 large chunks; place in bowl of KitchenAid stand mixer. Attach bowl and flat beater to mixer. Turn to Stir speed; mix until pork is shredded to desired consistency. Return to Dutch oven; stir to coat with juices. Serve on buns with coleslaw and barbecue sauce, if desired.

Garlic and Herb Pork Sausage

MAKES ABOUT 8 SAUSAGES

2 pounds boneless pork shoulder, cut into 1½-inch cubes

½ pound pork belly, cut into 1½-inch cubes

½ pound pork fatback, cut into 1½-inch cubes

2½ teaspoons sea salt

1 teaspoon freshly ground black pepper

3 cloves garlic

2 teaspoons chopped fresh thyme

2 teaspoons chopped fresh parsley

1 teaspoon chopped fresh rosemary

1 teaspoon red pepper flakes

2 teaspoons white wine

4 feet natural* or synthetic sausage casing

1 tablespoon olive oil

*Soak natural casings in cold water at least 30 minutes before using; rinse thoroughly.

1 Line baking sheet with parchment paper. Place pork on prepared baking sheet; freeze 20 minutes. Season with salt and pepper.

2 Assemble KitchenAid food grinder with coarse grinding plate; attach to KitchenAid stand mixer. Place mixer bowl under grinder. Turn mixer to speed 4; grind pork shoulder, pork belly, fatback, garlic and herbs into bowl, taking care not to force it through.

3 Remove food grinder; attach flat beater to mixer. Add red pepper flakes and wine to meat mixture. Turn to speed 2; mix 2 to 3 minutes or until well blended.

4 Attach KitchenAid sausage stuffer with large stuffing tube to mixer. Grease tube with olive oil or water; slide casing on tightly and tie end. Turn mixer to speed 4; slowly feed sausage mixture into hopper using food pusher. Hold tied end of casing in one hand and guide pork mixture as it fills casing. Do not pack too tightly in casing. Twist and shape sausages into 4- to 5-inch links as you go. Separate sausages and refrigerate or freeze until ready to cook.

5 To cook, heat olive oil in large skillet or cast iron skillet over medium-high heat. Place sausage in skillet and brown on all sides. Reduce heat to low; cook 15 to 20 minutes or until cooked through (160°F).

6 To grill, heat grill to medium heat. Add sausage links; cook 5 minutes. Turn and cook an additional 5 minutes or until cooked through (160°F).

Sausage and Butternut Squash Lasagna Rolls

MAKES 8 ROLLS

PASTA

- 2 **cups 00 pasta flour or all-purpose flour**
- ¼ **teaspoon salt**
- 2 **eggs**
- 1 **teaspoon olive oil**
- 1 **to 2 tablespoons water**
  Semolina flour

FILLINGS

- 2 **cups cubed peeled butternut squash (½-inch pieces)**
- ½ **cup chopped sweet onion**
- 2 **cloves garlic, minced**
- 1 **tablespoon olive oil**
- 1 **pound sweet Italian sausage**
- 15 **ounces whole milk ricotta cheese**

- 1½ **cups chopped fresh spinach**
- ¾ **cup (3 ounces) shredded mozzarella cheese**
- 2 **tablespoons chopped fresh parsley**
  Salt and freshly ground black pepper

GARLIC SAGE BECHAMEL

- 3 **tablespoons unsalted butter**
- 3 **tablespoons all-purpose flour**
- 2¼ **cups whole milk**
- 1 **clove garlic**
- ¼ **cup fresh sage leaves**
- ¾ **cup grated Parmesan cheese**
- 1½ **cups (5 ounces) shredded mozzarella cheese, divided**
  Salt and freshly ground black pepper

1 Place pasta flour and ¼ teaspoon salt in bowl of KitchenAid stand mixer. Attach bowl and flat beater to mixer. Turn to speed 2; mix 30 seconds. Make a well in the center of flour mixture; add eggs and 1 teaspoon olive oil. Turn to speed 2; mix 2 minutes. Add water 1 tablespoon at a time until dough holds together. Replace flat beater with dough hook. Turn to Stir speed; knead 2 to 3 minutes. Shape dough into a ball; wrap in plastic wrap and let rest at least 1 hour.

2 Attach KitchenAid pasta roller to mixer with adjustment knob set to 1. Divide dough into quarters and flatten one piece, keeping remaining dough wrapped to prevent drying out. Turn mixer to speed 2 and feed flattened dough through rollers to knead. Fold dough in half and roll again, repeating until dough is smooth and pliable and covers the width of the rollers. Change roller setting to 2 and feed dough sheet through rollers to flatten; do not fold dough for this step. Repeat for roller settings 3 to 5. Lay dough on work surface; lightly dust with semolina flour. Cut each piece in half crosswise. Cover lightly with plastic wrap.

3 Preheat oven to 400°F. Combine butternut squash, onion and minced garlic in 13×9-inch baking pan. Drizzle with 1 tablespoon olive oil; toss to coat. Roast 15 to 20 minutes or until squash is fork tender and beginning to brown. *Reduce oven temperature to 375°F.*

4 Meanwhile, heat large skillet over medium-high heat. Add sausage; cook 5 to 7 minutes or until cooked through, breaking up sausage with wooden spoon. Add to squash; stir to combine. Combine ricotta, spinach, ¾ cup mozzarella, parsley, ½ teaspoon salt and ½ teaspoon pepper in large bowl. Set sausage mixture and ricotta mixture aside.

5 For sauce, melt butter in medium saucepan over low heat. Whisk in all-purpose flour; cook 2 to 3 minutes or until light golden, whisking constantly. Gradually whisk in milk in thin steady stream; stir in garlic clove and sage leaves. Cook 3 to 4 minutes or until thickened, whisking constantly. Remove and discard garlic and sage leaves. Remove from heat; stir in Parmesan and ¼ cup mozzarella until smooth and well blended. Season with ½ teaspoon salt and ½ teaspoon pepper.

6 Bring large pot of salted water to a boil over high heat. Add four strips of pasta at a time; cook 3 minutes. Remove pasta from water with tongs and drain in colander. Rinse under cold water until cool enough to handle; lay on work surface.

7 Grease 13×9-inch baking pan lightly with olive oil. Spread ricotta mixture evenly over noodles; top evenly with sausage mixture, pressing down slightly. Roll up noodles and place in prepared pan. Pour sauce over rolls; sprinkle with remaining 1 cup mozzarella. Bake 30 to 40 minutes or until heated through and edges are crisp. Serve immediately.

Attachment Index

Flat Beater (continued)

Honey-Pecan Coffee Cake, 158

Key Lime Pie, 54

Lemon Cream Dessert, 90

Lemon Squares, 34

Loaded Banana Bread, 126

Mango Lime Galettes, 46

Mexican Hot Chocolate Cookies, 20

Mixed Berry Almond Cake, 70

Monkey Bread, 116

Multigrain Loaf, 114

Parmesan-Herb Bagels, 120

Peanut Butter and Jelly Bars, 38

Peanut Butter Pie, 48

Pull-Apart Potato Rolls, 110

Pulled Pork, 180

Pumpkin Cheesecake, 72

Pumpkin Cheesecake Bars, 32

Raspberry Tart, 50

Raspberry White Chocolate Cheesecake, 62

Red Velvet Cake, 76

Rhubarb Bread, 132

Sausage and Butternut Squash Lasagna Rolls, 184

Sea Salt Chocolate Chunk Cookies, 18

Shortbread Turtle Cookie Bars, 36

Six-Layer Chocolate Cake, 78

Sour Cream Coffee Cake, 154

Flat Beater (continued)

Steamed Pork Buns, 172

Super Chocolate Cookies, 24

Toasted Coconut Doughnuts, 140

Tomato Basil Tart, 166

Vegan Chocolate Cake, 60

Food Grinder

Garlic and Herb Pork Sausage, 182

Merguez Sausage, 162

Ice Cream Maker

Pumpkin Ice Cream with Pistachio Brittle, 96

Pasta Roller

Fettuccine with Heirloom Tomatoes, Burrata and Balsamic, 164

Sausage and Butternut Squash Lasagna Rolls, 184

Sausage Stuffer

Garlic and Herb Pork Sausage, 182

Merguez Sausage, 162

Spiralizer

Apple Clafoutis, 88

Focaccia with Squash and Olives, 112

Spiralizer (continued)

Pear Salad with Blue Cheese Dressing, 168

Wire Whip

Boston Cream Cupcakes, 64

Carrot Cake, 68

Chocolate Mousse, 86

Cookies and Cream Sheet Cake, 74

Deep-Dish Ham Quiche, 174

Éclair Cake, 94

Eggs Benedict, 178

Gingerbread Whoopie Pies, 14

Lemon Cream Dessert, 90

Lemon Squares, 34

Madeleines, 8

Peanut Butter Pie, 48

Sponge Cake with Passionfruit Topping, 82

Vegan Chocolate Cake, 60

Warm Chocolate Soufflé Cakes, 92

Recipe Index

Metric Conversion Chart

VOLUME MEASUREMENTS (dry)

$1/8$ teaspoon = 0.5 mL
$1/4$ teaspoon = 1 mL
$1/2$ teaspoon = 2 mL
$3/4$ teaspoon = 4 mL
1 teaspoon = 5 mL
1 tablespoon = 15 mL
2 tablespoons = 30 mL
$1/4$ cup = 60 mL
$1/3$ cup = 75 mL
$1/2$ cup = 125 mL
$2/3$ cup = 150 mL
$3/4$ cup = 175 mL
1 cup = 250 mL
2 cups = 1 pint = 500 mL
3 cups = 750 mL
4 cups = 1 quart = 1 L

VOLUME MEASUREMENTS (fluid)

1 fluid ounce (2 tablespoons) = 30 mL
4 fluid ounces ($1/2$ cup) = 125 mL
8 fluid ounces (1 cup) = 250 mL
12 fluid ounces ($1^1/2$ cups) = 375 mL
16 fluid ounces (2 cups) = 500 mL

WEIGHTS (mass)

$1/2$ ounce = 15 g
1 ounce = 30 g
3 ounces = 90 g
4 ounces = 120 g
8 ounces = 225 g
10 ounces = 285 g
12 ounces = 360 g
16 ounces = 1 pound = 450 g

DIMENSIONS

$1/16$ inch = 2 mm
$1/8$ inch = 3 mm
$1/4$ inch = 6 mm
$1/2$ inch = 1.5 cm
$3/4$ inch = 2 cm
1 inch = 2.5 cm

OVEN TEMPERATURES

250°F = 120°C
275°F = 140°C
300°F = 150°C
325°F = 160°C
350°F = 180°C
375°F = 190°C
400°F = 200°C
425°F = 220°C
450°F = 230°C

BAKING PAN SIZES

Utensil	Size in Inches/Quarts	Metric Volume	Size in Centimeters
Baking or	8×8×2	2 L	20×20×5
Cake Pan	9×9×2	2.5 L	23×23×5
(square or	12×8×2	3 L	30×20×5
rectangular)	13×9×2	3.5 L	33×23×5
Loaf Pan	8×4×3	1.5 L	20×10×7
	9×5×3	2 L	23×13×7
Round Layer	8×$1^1/2$	1.2 L	20×4
Cake Pan	9×$1^1/2$	1.5 L	23×4
Pie Plate	8×$1^1/4$	750 mL	20×3
	9×$1^1/4$	1 L	23×3
Baking Dish	1 quart	1 L	—
or Casserole	$1^1/2$ quart	1.5 L	—
	2 quart	2 L	—